Freedom of the Self

Freedom of the Self

*Kenosis, Cultural Identity, and Mission
at the Crossroads*

Jeffrey F. Keuss

PICKWICK *Publications* · Eugene, Oregon

FREEDOM OF THE SELF
Kenosis, Cultural Identity, and Mission at the Crossroads

Pickwick Publications
An Imprint of Wipf and Stock Publishers
199 W. 8th Ave., Suite 3
Eugene, OR 97401

www.wipfandstock.com

ISBN 13: 978-1-60899-105-1

Cataloging-in-Publication data:

Keuss, Jeffrey F.

    Freedom of the self : kenosis, cultural identity, and mission at the crossroads / Jeffrey F. Keuss.

    x + 172 p. ; 23 cm. Includes bibliographical references and indexes.

    ISBN 13: 978-1-60899-105-1

    1. Self-denial. 2. Group identity. 3. Missions. 4. Church. 5. Christianity and culture. I. Title.

BX2350.2 .K45 2010

Manufactured in the U.S.A.

Dedicated to my parents Jeff and Sandra
who have journeyed with me in times both light and dark

Contents

Acknowledgments

WRITING IS AN ACT of remembrance—breathing new life into long forgotten lives and ideas so that they may reanimate yet another generation. As with writing, so is life as an act of deep remembrance. Much of who I am as a scholar and teacher is the result of being remembered well by many people.

In particular, my immediate thanks to my colleagues in the School of Theology at Seattle Pacific University as well as the Center for Scholarship and Faculty Development, who provided course release time and funding to bring this project to completion. When chapter 11 of the Letter to the Hebrews in the New Testament lists the litany of names that exemplify faith, I count my colleagues at SPU among those implied. For "such a cloud of witnesses" I am truly blessed. Much of the preliminary review of the manuscript was done by Raoul Perez, Caitlin Rohl, and John Harrell, who are tireless SPU students and wonderful reading partners. Additionally, my deep thanks to my wife, Diana, and my daughters Clara, Eilidh, and Miriam, whose love coupled with quick wit and gracious wonder is a gift without parallel.

My thanks also to the following publications for granting permission to revise earlier work into the book you have before you: chapter 3 is largely drawn from an earlier article entitled "Seeing and Being with Youth: *Bildungsroman* and Coming of Age from Goethe to *Star Wars* and *The Matrix*" (*Journal of Youth and Theology* 2.5 [December 2006] 29–46). Portions of chapter 4 were drawn from an earlier article entitled "The Emergent Church and Neo-correlational Theology after Tillich, Schliermacher and Browning" (*Scottish Journal of Theology* 61.4 [2008] 450–61). Chapter 5 drew together some work published as both a revision of a much earlier article entitled "*Differánce* as One Who Comes Unknown: Christology after Derrida's 'Structure, Sign, and Play in the Discourse of the Human Sciences'" (*Journal for Cultural and Religious Theory* 3.1 [December 2001] n.p.) as well as a revision of material I published in a chapter entitled "Turning a Blind Eye: Emmanuel Levinas, John 9 and the Blindness of Responsibility" (in *The Bible in World Christian Perspective*, ed. David W. Baker and W. Ward Gasque, 175–92; Vancouver: Regent College Publishing, 2009). Chapter 6 is a revision of an earlier article that originally appeared as "The Lenten Face of Christ in Shusaku Endo's *Silence* and *Life of Jesus*" (*Expository Times* 118.6 [March 2007] 273–79). Chapter 8 saw its first life as part of a theme issue looking at economics, and was entitled "The New Poverty and Responsive Economics" (*The Other Journal* 2.5 [April 4, 2005] n.p.).

Lastly, I dedicate this project to my parents Jeff and Sandra. To spend years reflecting on the nature of identity formation without giving a humble nod to those who made this life possible for me would defeat much of what I have been arguing for. Their love through the years in both times of darkness and light have freed me to think, to laugh, to weep, and to celebrate what it is to strive toward the life of the kenotic self I have written about within both the covers of this book you now hold and the life I continue to strive for each day.

Introduction

You Are What You Love—the Kenotic Self

THOSE WHO HAVE SEEN many of the seventeenth-century Dutch master Rembrandt's works will agree that "The Nightwatch" stands as one of his masterpieces. It is a truly stunning canvas. As you walk to the top of a central staircase in the Rijksmuseum, you see this massive work gently illuminated with dappled light falling through the ceiling panels. It depicts a group of city guardsmen awaiting the command to fall in line. Each person is painted with the care that Rembrandt gave to single individual portraits, yet the composition is such that the separate figures are second in interest to the effect of the whole. The canvas is brilliant with color, movement, and light. In the foreground are two men, one in bright yellow, the other in black. The shadow of one color tones down the lightness of the other. In the center of the painting is a little girl dressed in yellow. You cannot take your eyes off the painting as it fills your vision to the periphery. What is striking at first sight is the sheer size and spectacle of the work, but within seconds you are drawn to the blending of particular individuals framed as a whole. Stepping back a bit further, you will note a gorgeous gilded frame around the painting.

There is a story about "The Nightwatch" that I heard while viewing it a few years ago in Amsterdam, which serves to frame—both literally and figuratively—the discussion that is to follow. When Rembrandt was commissioned to do the painting, a frame was built in anticipation for the completed work. As things often go, the frame was completed months prior to the painting itself. As the painting was placed in relation to the frame, a problem became evident—the length of the frame was three feet shorter than the painting itself. To resolve this dilemma, a rather remarkable move was made: the painting's edge was cut by three feet so that it could fit the frame. There is certainly an air of the apocryphal to this story, and the guide at the museum underscored this point, but the sheer possibility sent shivers down my spine. How could someone standing before such a masterpiece ever conceive that choosing the gilded frame over and against the unity of the composition was a viable option? Yet theology has done this time and time again—favoring doctrinal method and form that delimits and at times violates the very thing that theological method is hoping to adequately "frame" and celebrate.

To this end it is my hope to correct a trajectory in certain circles of theological discussion that seems quick to cut away core concerns of the faith in the attempt to defend certain doctrines without considering the larger picture. In short, this book is concerned with the loss of the self amidst what is happening in the Emergent and missional discussions. This is not a concern isolated to or indicative of Emergent or missional conversations *per se*, but it is a loss that undermines the very heartbeat of the good I see being offered in the Emergent and missional reformation discussions within contemporary theological and ministerial discourse. What I am arguing for throughout the pages that follow is a manifesto of sorts, a trumpeting to return to a deeper sense of what it means to be an authentic self in the world—a return to what I am terming "the kenotic self." While the challenge to Christendom brought forth in the current Emergent dialogues spearheaded by Brian McLaren, Tony Jones, and others has looked toward the event horizon of a reformed ecclesiology and a concern for the "other," it is my hope that embracing the kenotic self as seen throughout this book will provide a deep model for authentic personhood in our time and the age to come. It is time to consider the full canvas of our humanity once again.

CONTOURS OF THE EMERGENT MOVEMENT

The "Emergent movement" is the collective term for those within Western culture who continue to find community together amidst a process of the theological and subjective deconstruction and reconstruction of Christianity. Emerging church groups have typically possessed some or all of the following characteristics:

1. A minimalist and decentralized organizational structure.

2. A flexible and at times mongrel approach to theology whereby individual differences in belief and morality are celebrated and accepted, with difference as normative.

3. A holistic view of the role of the church in society. This can mean anything from greater emphasis on fellowship in the structure of the group to a higher degree of emphasis on social action, community building, or Christian outreach.

4. A desire to reanalyze the Bible against its context with the goal of revealing a multiplicity of valid perspectives rather than a single valid interpretation.

5. A high value placed on creating communities built out of the creativity of those who are a part of each local body.

On the Emergent Village website, the word "emergent" is defined as "normally an adjective meaning coming into view, arising from, occurring unexpectedly, requiring immediate action (hence its relation to 'emergency'), characterized by evolutionary emergence, or crossing a boundary (as between water and air)." They further define the Emergent community through four key terms:

1. "Growing": which indicates a desire to develop as the dreams of God for the healing, redemption, and reconciliation of the world develop.

2. "Generative": which means to expect friendships to generate new ideas, connections, opportunities, and works of beauty.

3. "Friendship": that living in reconciled friendship is the priority that often will trump traditional orthodoxies—indeed, orthodoxy requires reconciliation as a prerequisite.

4. "Missional": that the call of the Gospel is an outward, apostolic call into the world.[1]

This multivaliant approach to grounding an operational definition for the Emerging church only serves to accentuate this anti-movement movement and diminishes the place of the self amidst the exaltation of the collective. A recent master's thesis analyzing the Emerging church movement operationally defined the phrase "emerging church" as a "mood, generative conversation, dialogue, phenomenon, and even as a friendship amongst its church leaders that share common features."[2] Consider the

---

1. http://www.emergentvillage.com/about/.
2. Flores, "Exploration."

following response from a pastor asked to define what it means to be an Emergent church:

> emerging church is a passion for people who are stuck with a congregation of people who don't understand half of what they say. The emergent movement has indeed emerged from the big stone doors of the so-called local church to move themselves (usually [*sic*] a 18–30's group) down the road to the pub. The emerging church can now express themselves in the language they use (graphics, candles, trance music, beer, whatever) . . . to me, that's what it seems to be. It's a radical redecoration, break up all the furniture and stick it back together again, take all the bits done within a church setting and make them make sense for their generation, their cultural context.[3]

This "radical redecoration" includes an embrace of paradox and uncertainty in regard to:

1. a constantly changing philosophical understanding of subjectivity— from modern to postmodern, from a world of absolutes and certainty to a world of questions and searching, of challenge and anxiety, of opportunity and danger;

2. constantly changing social and economic systems in the midst of a growing global economy and the rise of the Internet and other global media, which make the world seem smaller and more connected, yet also more fragmented and tense; and

3. a rabid embrace of constantly changing spiritualities, as religions of the world cope with new challenges and opportunities, religious and ethnic strife, the loss of confidence in traditional authorities, and the shift of Christianity's strength from the global North to the global South.

FROM EMERGENT TO MISSIONAL AND BACK AGAIN . . .

How does the notion of the Emerging church as described above intersect with the Christian notion of being about the "mission of God"? Often the term "mission" is used to denote a certain type of sending out—"I am going to _____ on a mission"—or of activity being engaged in—"I am a missionary to college students." Recently the term "mission" has been fur-

---

3. Dodridge, "I Am Not."

4

ther defined as the core of what the church is to be in and for the world, as in the phrase "missional church," put forward by key missiologists such as Darrell Guder, George Hunsberger, and Craig Van Gelder.[4] This is a notion of sending, of "going out" from where the church *is* to where the church is *called to be*. In the end of Matthew's Gospel, this (com)mission is placed before the disciples, which we now refer to as the "Great Commission":

> Then Jesus came to them and said, "All authority in heaven and on earth has been given to me. Therefore go and make disciples of all nations, baptizing them in the name of the Father and of the Son and of the Holy Spirit, and teaching them to obey everything I have commanded you. And surely I am with you always, to the very end of the age."[5]

As the church has heard this (com)mission, a veritable stampede of missional activity has ensued as the core mandate to "therefore go and make disciples" has been embraced.

It is this notion of the missional church that has grounded some of the discussions in Emergent circles and defined the primary theological loci of the church as a "going out" rather than a "staying in" people that underscores much of the work by key Emergent voices. As argued by Brian McLaren in *More Ready Than You Realize*,[6] throughout the centuries of reflection on the activity and method by which the Christian message has been proclaimed and incarnated in the world, this central point—that *mission was never about drawing people to the church alone but a journey of going out into all the world*—seems either to have been assumed and then ignored, or merely overlooked as a point of responsible and humble repose in evangelistic practice. For McLaren, the task of the church is to go out into the entire world and participate in God's work through "conversation, as friendship, as influence, as invitation, as companionship, as challenge, as opportunity, as conversation, as dance, as something you get to do."[7] In short, McLaren rightly argues that the church has become so enmeshed in its self-preservation that it has lost its ability to even com-

---

4. See titles in The Gospel and Our Culture Series, such as Guder, ed., *Missional Church*; and Hunsberger and Van Gelder, eds., *Church between Gospel and Culture*.

5. Matt 28:18–20.

6. McLaren, *More Ready*.

7. Ibid., 5.

municate the gospel in which it has been grounded—a message of Good News that only finds purchase when shared, not when hoarded. In this regard much of what has become known as "missions" is nothing but self-definition and self-assurance rather than proclamation.

Part of this is due to the "mission industry" that arose in the dawn of the twentieth century and has solidified in the wake of the World Wars, which continues to both inspire and plague the message of the gospel. One need only look to the recent cultural reimaginings of missionaries in such works as Barbara Kingsolver's *The Poisonwood Bible* and Peter Matthiessen's *At Play in the Fields of the Lord* to see that even with supposedly good mission work taking place, the verdict on the efficacy of Christian mission is that it has been found, for lack of a better word, wanting.

Granted, conversations surrounding missional theology within the fairly new discipline of mission studies have moved in some exciting directions since the publication of David J. Bosch's seminal *Transforming Mission: Paradigm Shifts in Theology of Mission* over a decade ago. It was Bosch's deep reading of Scripture coupled with his profound appreciation of cultural studies that led him to the conviction that the shape of the gospel was missional:

> Mission [is] understood as being derived from the very nature of God. It [is] thus put in the context of the doctrine of the Trinity, not of ecclesiology or soteriology. The classical doctrine of the *missio Dei* as God the Father sending the Son, and God the Father and the Son sending the Spirit [is] expanded to include yet another "movement": Father, Son, and Holy Spirit sending the church into the world.[8]

Competing Themes in Contemporary Missiology

But while Bosch's Trinitarian rendering of the *missio Dei* alerts us to the dynamic calling and form of missions, this is not the dynamic image seen in most missional endeavors today. As noted by missiologist Paul Hiebert,[9] three major themes or *raisons d'être* continue to strive for primacy within the modern missiology movement after Bosch.

---

8. Bosch, *Transforming Mission*, 390.

9. Hiebert, "Evangelism," 153.

I. Evangelism

Without evangelism, this first camp will argue, there will be no visible church and no manifestation of the kingdom of God in places where the gospel has never been preached. This conviction has motivated missionaries to go to "unevangelized" peoples at all ends of the earth, giving their lives so that all might hear and believe. The obvious strengths of this emphasis include the ability to articulate the purpose of the church coupled with a posture that is outward looking. However, weaknesses of this emphasis include:

- *Little deepening of relationship, plus a lack of concern for people beyond initial commitment.* This is manifested in "touring"—missionaries "on the move," trying to contact as many as possible without engaging relationally.

- *A flawed ecclesiology.* Little attention is given to churches becoming mature communities of faith; development of worship, fellowship, ministry, leadership, and discipleship is left to others. The church is a holding pen until the second coming.

- *An individualistic salvation*; it only has to do with a person's relationship to God, but not to the community or to the larger world. Faith is privatized and spiritualized. Success or failure is dependent on the number of converts, not on transformed lives or transformed conditions. Issues such as peace and justice, among others, are deemed secondary. As E. Stanley Jones succinctly put it, "An individual gospel without a social gospel is a soul without a body, and a social gospel without an individual gospel is a body without a soul. One is a ghost and the other a corpse. Put the two together, and you have a living person."[10]

II. Church

Here the emphasis is placed on the priority of the church as the agent and goal of missions. Christ is preparing the church as a covenant community, which gathers to worship God, strengthen believers, and carry out evangelism. The task of missions, therefore, is to build the church. To do so, we must organize congregations, train leaders, and nurture children in the faith. In this emphasis it is the church that preserves the gospel from

---

10. Jones, *Song of Ascents*, 151.

generation to generation despite opposition and persecution. Strengths of this model include a rich and robust concern (greater than under the Evangelism model) for the importance of the worshipping community. Additionally, there is a vital importance placed on spiritual growth and on grounding the community of faith. Weaknesses of this model include:

1. *The danger of an inward focus, of becoming "ingrown,"* such as what has happened to the evangelical movement in North America. Institutionalization demanded more and more resources, which resulted in a more congregational focus. Many evangelical churches maintained the rhetoric of evangelism, but in practice assigned their resources and best personnel to minister within the church. Evangelism became one of many projects.

2. *The approach mirrors a humanist focus.* Everything is done by our efforts alone: *we* build churches, *we* produce programs, *we* create activities. There is little room for input from those other than us.

III. KINGDOM

Here the kingdom of God is the focus and central theme of missions. Conversion and church are seen not as ends unto themselves, but as means of proclaiming the kingdom of God that is already come. The mantra of this model is that in the New Testament Jesus refers to the kingdom of God over a hundred times. In this model the clear central task of the church is to proclaim justice and peace in a world full of oppression and war; the Good News of the kingdom is that the gospel is here and now. Strengths of this model include a deep concern for righteousness on earth and its view of mission as something that is continuous and all-encompassing— something not completed until the kingdom is realized in full throughout all creation, until God's peace and reconciliation is fulfilled on earth as it is in heaven. Weaknesses of this model include:

- *The potential of losing sight of the spiritual "lostness" of human beings without Christ.* As noted by missiologist Arthur Glasser, "The church has never been so harassed and troubled by voices calling for a reduction or abandonment of evangelism—and for the reconceptualization of its message and mission in terms of social justice and international peace."[11]

---

11. Glasser, *Announcing the Kingdom.*

- *The church becomes merely another political player in the arena of world politics.* The church is no longer either a countercultural community or a prophetic voice. In this regard Christianity becomes just another social program or (at best) a civil religion used only to *justify* democracy, capitalism, individual rights, or Western civilization rather than to *give meaning to and/or question* such things.

Do we hold on to a missional mindset amidst these competing trends or do we move missions to the secondary task of the church behind the more important goal of establishing a presence? There is a crisis in missions on a number of fronts:

- *Definition*: What is mission?

- *Conviction*: Why mission?

- *Authority*: Mission? . . . On whose authority?

- *Responsibility*: Whose mission?

Despite these challenges, the call to develop a thoroughly missional ecclesiology that embraces and supports the development of the self is vital. As will be seen throughout this book, the challenge is to keep both the mission of God as other-focused and yet still attend to the needs of the emerging self. As has been so often stated, it is not the church of God who has a mission in the world—it is the God of mission who has a church in the world. What are some of the contours of this missional community that supports the development of the self? A *missional ecclesiology* reminds us to consider the following.

Contours of an Emergent Missional Ecclesiology

The Role of Scripture

Much of what fills the pages of books and seminars concerned with new models of church seems utterly devoid of scriptural reflection. Scripture has been central to the great reformations of the church and continues to be its authoritative bedrock. As noted by Darrell Guder, "Whatever one believes about the church needs to be found in and based on what the Bible teaches. Moreover, these biblical perspectives need to be made explicit. The biblical witness is appropriately received as the testimony to

God's mission and the formation of God's missionary people to be the instruments and witness of that mission."[12]

THE ROLE OF HISTORY

The gathering of God's people is a deeply contextualized and historically grounded reality. Granted, it occurs in an ever present Now, but its eschatological shape is bound in the fullness of time—both past and future impinge upon the Now and give the people of God its form and meaning. Guder states it succinctly: "When we shape our ecclesiology for a particular culture, we must take into consideration the historical development of other ecclesiologies. Today this means reading our Western history and the worldwide emergence of the church carefully. As part of our catholicity, we are guided by the Christian church in all its cultural expressions, those that precede us and those that are contemporary with us."[13]

THE ROLE OF CONTEXT

As noted in the previous paragraph, every ecclesiology or model of the church is developed within a particular cultural context. Darrell Guder's injunction is to remember that "the gospel is always translated into a culture, and God's people are formed in that culture in response to the translated and Spirit-empowered Word. All ecclesiologies function relative to their context. Their truth and faithfulness are related both to the gospel they proclaim and to the witness they foster in every culture."[14]

TO BE ESCHATOLOGICAL

With Jürgen Moltmann's seminal work *Theology of Hope*, we are challenged to remember that eschatology is not a statement of possibility but an affirmation of promise in the reality of hope in the Now. As he states, "faith takes its stand on hope and 'hastens beyond this world' [as noted by John Calvin]. [Calvin] did not mean by this that Christian faith flees the world, but he did mean that it strains after the future. To believe does in fact mean to cross and transcend bounds, to be engaged in an exodus. Yet this happens in a way that does not suppress or skip the unpleasant realities."[15] To be missionally concerned is then to be straining for the

12. Guder, "Missional Church," 11.

13. Ibid.

14. Ibid.

15. Moltmann, *Theology of Hope*, 19.

promise amidst the "unpleasant reality" of our current context. As Darrell Guder challenges us, we are to then see our lives as

> developmental and dynamic in nature, if we believe the church is the work of the creating and inspiring Spirit of God and is moving toward God's promised consummation of all things. *Neither the church nor its interpretive doctrine may be static.* New biblical insights will convert the church and its theology; new historical challenges will raise questions never before considered; and new cultural contexts will require a witnessing response that redefines how we function.[16]

This is a truly grand vision for the body of Christ. That said, as the focus has continued to situate the mission of God (*missio Dei*) as an exclusively corporate activity, there remains a loss to and for the individual as a unique, unrepeatable miracle of God. This is the challenge to individuals formed after the Enlightenment: to think of themselves as a subject before the Living God prior to their realignment of self as part of the body of Christ. In this regard, our understanding of self is distanced from our understanding of the mission of God and our place as individual subjects. If evangelism is a call to the individual and mission is the work of the church, the individual is only partially commissioned in and for the full *missio Dei*. In that regard, this book will attempt to return the notion of *missio Dei* to the core defining principle of what it means to be a self in and for the world. As the subsequent chapters of this book outline, the idea of the kenotic self as a missionally active subject in and for the world is deeply imbedded in the Christian tradition, given that the identity we have as subjects is found and forged not in doctrine *per se* but in Christ. As Graham Ward has rightly asserted in *Christ and Culture*, "Christological discourse was born not simply for catechesis but for mission."[17] In short, to speak of Christ at all—let alone ourselves as subjects—is to speak "onto-missionally" ("I am") rather than doctrinally or even creedally. We will begin by looking at how the understanding of the self as a moral agent through the work of St. Augustine and Aristotle calls this view of the self to the foreground. Additionally, we will look at some new dialogue partners and sources of theological reflection and method from the field of Continental philosophy, who are welcome voices in the move toward a dynamic missional focus of the self for twenty-first-century theology.

16. Guder, "Missional Church," 12; emphasis added.

17. Ward, *Christ and Culture*, 17.

OUTLINE OF THIS STUDY

Three major goals will be addressed through the chapters that are to follow:

- Finding a language for the kenotic self that is in concert with the core of the Emergent movement as well as being deeply missional, and that includes an acknowledgement of lament, terror, and violence after a century of global warfare and genocide amidst the claims of the Good News.

- An honest and humble awareness of otherness in the face of multicultural and multifaith dialogue, while still proclaiming the call toward "one Lord, one faith, one baptism," that shapes how we understand what it means to be a self in the world.

- A shift toward honest dialogue with non-Western writers such as Shusaku Endo toward a missional methodology of the self that finds common ground with faith traditions outside Western configurations of Christianity.

In this way, striving toward a model of the self as kenotic is an attempt at offering a nexus point for the Emergent movement, missional theology, and Continental philosophy that can enrich theological discussions and provide a viable middle way between many of the static theologies that have proved problematic for evangelism and mission in truly embracing the depth and radical nature of the Great Commission. Rather than look for ways to fit the canvas of our humanity within preconceived, ready-at-hand frames, the very nature of a kenotic approach is to overflow expectations, boundaries, and limitations—to view fully rather than frame that which we are called to behold. What is clear throughout the following chapters is a renewed appreciation for what Continental thought offers in a reengagement with a kenotic approach to personhood as an appeal for a missiology of the self. This is a fluid, moving sense of identity framed as a metaphysics of love to be released into and for the sake of the Gospel of Jesus Christ.

In short, it is my hope that this return to a view of identity in light of the kenotic call is a stimulating, thoughtful, and deeply practical reflection on how the church lives and moves and has its being in the twenty-first century.

PART ONE

The Movement of the Self

Scripture and the Kenotic Self

A Deep Reading of Philippians 2

"I CAN'T LIVE, WITH OR WITHOUT YOU"

P OPULAR MUSIC SINCE THE late 1960s has been replete with claims
of what it means to have identity in the world. Whether our sense
of identity is bound up in the longing for love, the loss of our past, or
the social injustice that removes people from seeing their true beauty
and worth, popular music has made its mark on how much of Western
culture thinks about itself. In 1987, the Irish rock band U2 released what
has been one of the most celebrated rock albums in history—*The Joshua
Tree*. Where most of the popular music released in the 1980s was filled
with claims of the self framed by needing more and more—more things
("I am a material girl in a material world"), more experiences ("Girls just
want to have fun"), more energy ("I want a new drug, one that won't make
me sick") and even more time ("Gotta get back in time"[1])—U2 produced
an album that was sparse in both its sonic and lyrical landscape. The lead
single, "With or without You," is a song of longing to be alive, yet the reso-
lution to this longing is not to be found in the accumulation of material
wealth or experiences, or even in just having more time. Rather, the singer
comes to the realization that to be fully alive will require binding his life
to the one he loves, and in doing so, he will end any sense of selfhood he
had previously known or aspired to. Approximately three minutes into
the song, as the protagonist wails in both lament and exaltation the refrain

---

1. These lines are from Madonna's "Material Girl" (*Like a Virgin*, 1983), Cyndi
Lauper's "Girls Just Want to Have Fun" (*She's So Unusual*, 1984), and Huey Lewis & the
News's "I Want a New Drug" (*Sports*, 1983) and "Back in Time" (*Back to the Future*, 1985),
respectively.

"I can't live, with or without you," lead singer Bono moves from mere words into something beyond categories—the sonic representation of Edvard Munch's 1893 painting "The Scream." With this release of the self into the sound beyond mere words, this simple pop song points toward much of what follows in this chapter, exploring what we will consider as the return to the call of the kenotic self. Is what it means to be in the world either about gathering things to our self—people, experiences, material possessions, knowledge—as an accumulating mode that ever increases and never relinquishes? Or are we merely to absolve everything, put the responsibility on mentors, doctrines, traditions, and take no responsibility for our lives? Both paths in absolute will be our death. Yet there is another model for what it means to be human offered forth in the New Testament through the life and ministry of Jesus—the way of the kenotic self.

Much of what constitutes self-awareness—knowing who I am and who you are—is often created out of cultural binaries and affixed to individuals and groups in a bricolage[2] composite—normal vs. odd, clean vs. dirty, intelligent vs. ignorant—in order to substantiate our perceived identity. One of the grand challenges of cultural identity formation is to acknowledge both the ongoing process by which our identity comes from such bricolage composites, and that we are called to something other than such formations. The danger is to perceive our identity as something that is either fixed or static (never changing; "just the way things are"), or perpetually and irrevocably out of our control by the whims and torrents of culture. Theorists such as Michel Foucault and Pierre Bourdieu[3] remind us how these perceived realities of identity fixity or constant change become implicit in the habits and/or structures of our daily lives. A discussion of Christ's kenotic nature becomes important theologically by offering that not only is our identity fluid rather than fixed, and therefore open to deepening change and redemption, but also that the actual presence of others is not fixed and static, but also fluid and available for intimacy rather than binary opposition. As the kenotic turn toward reconciliation within ourselves with and others is embraced as modeled by Christ's ex-

---

2. While there are a number of variant uses of "bricolage" in cultural theory, I am employing the term as the processes by which people acquire objects from across social divisions to create new cultural identities. Similar to creating a mosaic from broken shards of pottery, "bricolage" denotes the construction of cultural identity vis-à-vis the shards of culture ideology and taboo. See Lévi-Strauss, *Savage Mind*.

3. See Bourdieu, *Distinction*.

ample of the kenotic self, our lives take on the shape of a vocation (calling) of deep meaning. Rather than framed and fixed, we are to flow into the very reality of Christ, who opens himself to create a space where we can find intimacy and reconciliation.

Charles Wesley eloquently proclaimed in his hymn "And Can It Be" that to know and follow Christ is to acknowledge that he "emptied himself of all but love." "Kenosis" is a Greek term taken from Philippians 2:7, where Christ is spoken of as having "emptied himself" (NRSV) and taken human form. There has been much discussion about this entire crucial passage (2:6–11),[4] and several interpretations exist today. This chapter will provide a brief overview of the rise of kenotic theology,[5] with particular attention to an exegetical reading of Philippians 2 and its role in refocusing our attention on the person of Christ as the locus for a theological anthropology of the self in our work with youth in terms of some form of self-limitation by the pre-existent Son in becoming "Emmanuel"—"God-with-us."

"The kenotic turn," as the theological method discussed in this chapter, offers a model for Christian identity formation that places Christology as the locus of Christian faith by acknowledging that the primary concern for faith formation is to articulate a way of understanding the person of Christ that allowed his full humanity to be adequately expressed in light of his relinquishment of divine claim. Where critical scholarship surrounding Christology after the Left Hegelians (David F. Strauss, Ludwig Feuerbach) has been concerned with framing Jesus within the scientific method, new generations such as those seen in the Emergent conversations have accepted the limitations of that "prescientific" era and are willing to see the Synoptic portrait of the human personality of the man Jesus. There is therefore a need to acknowledge this renewed interest in

---

4. The scholarship surrounding the exegetical history of the *Carmen Christi* is expansive. While I will be referring to a number of key works, this paper primarily explores the philosophical and theological questions that arise from the kenotic tradition as they inform theological anthropology or the question of "being human" in relation to youth ministry education and practice. In addition to the many texts that will be cited throughout the paper, recent texts that have particularly informed this study are Evans, *Exploring Kenotic Christology*; Gorman, *Inhabiting the Cruciform God*; and Cronin, *Kenosis*.

5. Works such as those by Gottfried Thomasius (1802–75), Fairbairn, *Place of Christ in Modern Theology*; Gore, *Incarnation of the Son of God*; Garvie, *Studies in the Inner Life of Jesus*; and Forsyth, *Person and Place of Jesus Christ*, are key in the development kenotic theology in the modern period.

the kenotic Jesus as one who grew, hungered, learned, and appropriated his culture, as well as exhibiting its limitations through being truly human in it.

In his reflections on the New Testament and Kenosis Christology, New Testament scholar Gordon Fee notes that in his years of teaching, "evangelical students tended regularly to hold to a kind of naïve docetism, where Jesus appeared as a real person, but who was God in such a way that superseded anything truly human about him except for the accidents of his humanity—basically his bodily functions: eating, talking, sleeping, and so on."[6] This struggle for students to grasp the paradoxical gravity of Nicaea and Chalcedon—that Christ was truly, fully, completely human *and* truly, fully, completely God, and that Christ's expressions of hunger, longing, and sorrow were not some "accident of his humanity," as Fee's students ascertain, but rather the reality of Christ's life—is a deeply theological issue for those of us concerned with cultural identity formation. The struggle for Fee's students is essentially a lack of understanding what the kenotic emphasis of Christ calls us to and that kenosis is not merely an attribute for Christ alone to exemplify but is the very form of being for the continually sanctified disciple of Jesus.

Kenosis at its heart is a call upon the Christian to see the fulfillment of one's life, framed by the concerns of the kingdom of God as empowered by the Holy Spirit, not in accumulation but in relinquishment. In short, it is not what we have gained, but what we have forsaken that should be the theological key with which we sing "and they will know we are Christians by our love." As Fee makes clear in his assessment of the New Testament corpus, "the primary NT data that call for careful analysis, paying special attention to the way they speak about Christ's humanity . . . seem to express *some form of self-limitation of divine prerogatives on the part of the earthly Jesus*."[7]

Kenosis as "Making It Personal": Exegesis of Philippians 2:1–11

In Philippians 2, Paul seeks to reconcile the young church amidst their pagan context by challenging them on the one hand to "have the same mindset" with one another (ἀλλήλους / *allēlous*) that was in Christ, yet also implores them in verses 3–5 to "do nothing [μηδὲν / *mēden*] out of selfish ambition [ἐριθείαν / *eritheian*] or vain conceit [κενοδοξία / *keno-*

6. Fee, "New Testament and Kenosis Christology," 25.

7. Ibid., 29.

doxia; 'empty conceit/glory'], but in humility" place the concerns of others upon/within yourselves (ἀλλὰ καὶ τὰ ἑτέρων ἕκαστοι / *alla kai ta heterōn hekastoi*; "but make the things of others personal"). This call to "make things personal" is not a call to merely look beyond what divides us in ideology and power structures, to fashion some new utopian system that will replace a sinful system. No, this is a radical call to "get personal," to literally move into the lives of others and find habitation there, and conversely to create an expansive space of hospitality within our hearts and homes to allow and encourage others to be part of our family. In the days of the front porch in America, this was perhaps an easier thing—people could walk down a street and see the families who lived in the homes there talking in the evening, laughing, and perhaps crying together. We have largely become a nation—especially those of us in the middle-class—that has moved the family *from the porch to the patio*, putting our lives in the backyard, fenced in and closed off from others. Our churches have largely shown a similar shift: youth rooms pushed to the back rooms of labyrinthine church buildings, nurseries and children's rooms pushed away so crying does not distract worship, food banks work out of the back parking lot, and Alcohol Anonymous groups meeting after the "main church business" has concluded. By challenging the believers in Philippi to "make it personal," Paul is calling the church to move onto the porch, to be with each other. This is a call to cohabitation and existence within the space and orbit of each other that is more intimate than mere acknowledgment. In verse 5 Paul proceeds to set up the *Carmen Christi* of verses 6–11 by returning to the question of mindset from verse 2, stating that we are not only to adhere to the mindset of one another on the horizontal plane of *communitas*, but to adhere to the transcendent yet imminent way of Christ—we are to have the same mind (τοῦτο φρονεῖτε / *touto phroneite*; "this way to think") in us (ἐν ὑμῖν / *en hymin*; "in you") which is also in Christ Jesus (ὃ καὶ ἐν Χριστῷ Ἰησοῦ / *ho kai en Christō Iēsou*).

What follows in the *Carmen Christi*, the great song of Christ that Paul evokes in verses 6–11, frames two essential points by which the community of faith needs to frame itself: that as the form of God (μορφῇ θεοῦ / *morphē theou*) Christ emptied himself (ἐκένωσεν / *ekenōnsen*) by becoming human (6–7a), and secondly that as a human (ὁμοιώματι ἀνθρώπων γενόμενος καὶ σχήματι / *homoiōmati anthrōpōn genomenos kai schēmati*; "likeness of humans," and having become so in schema), Christ humbled himself (ἐταπείνωσεν ἑαυτὸν / *etapeinōsen heauton*) by becoming obedient unto death (θανάτου / *thanatou*). Therefore, in this *double humiliation*[8]—both as fully God and fully human—Christ is glorified (εἰς δόξαν θεοῦ πατρός / *eis doxan theou patros*; "to the glory of God the Father") which stands as a counterpoint to the vain conceit (κενοδοξία / *kenodoxia*; "empty conceit/glory") found in following the path of the pagan. Michael Gorman underscores this point of double humiliation by stating that Philippians 2 reminds us that

> Kenosis is thus the *sine qua non* ["without which (there is) nothing"] of both divinity and humanity, as revealed in the incarnation and cross of Christ, the one who was truly God and became human. His preexistent and incarnate actions [based on the literary and theological exegesis of Phil 2 show] essentially the same character. As Chalcedonian and therefore anachronistic as this claim will sound to some, it seems to be the inevitable conclusion of the line of thought we have been pursuing: it [Phil 2] is Chalcedon with a Pauline, cruciform twist.[9]

Yet is kenosis solely a divine attribute akin to omnipresence? In some translations, Philippians 2 translates μορφῇ θεοῦ / *morphē theou* as "the image of God" evoking εἰκὼν / *eikōn* as in Colossians 1:15, where Christ is called the εἰκὼν τοῦ θεοῦ τοῦ ἀοράτου / *eikōn tou theou tou aoratou* ("image of God invisible"). As Fee makes clear, "the reason for Paul's choice of μορφῇ [*morphē*] seems to be that it is the one word available in Greek that would fit two participial expressions on either side of the main verb (ἐκένωσεν); thus here it does not carry the sense of image (which it never carries, in any case), but refers rather to the essential quality of godliness, on the one hand, and of servanthood, on the other. But whatever else it is, it is not a synonym for εἰκὼν."[10] This use of μορφῇ / *morphē* is important in counterpoint to εἰκὼν, as noted by Fee, in that this "form" that is created by Christ is a "forming form," which we are called to inhabit and thereby become one with Christ and others.[11] As the Eastern church father John

---

8. I commend people to the song by Bill Mallonee (of the Vigilantes of Love) entitled "Double Cure" as a folk rock interpretation of this notion of "double humiliation."

9. Gorman, *Inhabiting the Cruciform God*, 36.

10. Fee, "New Testament and Kenosis Christology," 32.

11. The notion of "morphology" has deep historical importance for youth ministry education, and in particular the systematic raising of youth into adulthood in eighteenth-century Europe. "Morphology" was introduced into Western pedagogical traditions in the eighteenth century through the writings of Johann Wolfgang von Goethe and played a vital philosophical in the formation of the German notion of education as *bildung* (for-

Chrysostom reminds us in his homily on Philippians 2:5–8, "For nothing so sustains the great and philosophic soul in the performance of good works as learning that through this one is becoming like God."[12] What is evoked by Chrysostom is the movement of kenosis as theosis, where the emphasis "is on transformation by union, or participation, more than imitation, and is more appropriate than the language of imitation."[13] As Michael Gorman puts it, *"kenosis is theosis.* To be like Christ crucified is to be both most godly and most human. Christification is divinization, and divinization is humanization."[14] Therefore, kenosis is not exclusively the identity of God in isolation, rather the mark and form of God's union with us, and as such is the μορφῇ θεοῦ / *morphē theou* as the ever-forming form of God with the church for the sake of the world.

As seen in the kenotic turn of Christ that creates a forming form (μορφῇ θεοῦ / *morphē theou*) through the incarnation, we are offered a fully embodied manifestation of the God who is holy, yet not wholly genderless, raceless, and immune from the categories that define humanity. As such, our understanding of what it means to be human can (and should) be forged as much by the humanity of God in Christ as by the social sciences, which have provided a helpful supplement to theological anthropology over the years. A kenotic understanding of Christology offers us an undercurrent for deep identity formation: we are to take on the form of Christ, which calls us to manifest our humanity in the face of the particularity and alterity that arises in communal manifestations of the Body of Christ (1 Cor 12:12).

The theological challenge to how we see ourselves and others as human beings—as the *imago Dei* framed by the kenotic turn of Christ—is the realization that just seeing another as my brother or sister in Christ and repenting of my sinfulness does not preclude me from a journey of continued sanctification that leads into the kenotic form of Christ. Embracing identity formation in the shape and depth of the kenotic self that Christ affirms is a move of double humiliation: it is a release of that which I have seen God as being and doing in and for the world, in relation to my culturally formed identity, coupled with a move beyond

---

mation). For more on this tradition in relation to the *Bildungsroman*, see Keuss, "Seeing and Being."

12. John Chrysostom, *Homily on Philippians*, 7.2.5–8.

13. Gorman, *Inhabiting the Cruciform God*, 37.

14. Ibid.

self and into binding intimacy (John 15) that sacrifices systems, institutions, and power for the sake of deep and abiding relationship. What is underscored here in Philippians 2 is a clarion call beckoning us to listen to our lives as a symphonic response of complete relinquishment into Christ as the *morphē theou*, the "forming form of God" in and for the sake of the world.

In 1519, Hernán Cortés, the Castilian conquistador whose expedition to the Americas would eventually result in the fall of the Aztec empire, landed on the shores of the Americas and committed himself to the land with a move more radical than most missionaries: he set fire to the ships that carried him from Spain, committing himself fully to the Americas. Now, evoking Cortés may certainly seem antithetical to the cause of the gospel, but upholding his radical abandonment is not. In many respects the kenotic turn is a call to set fire to the ships and make our home in a place whether we live or die. Another way to say this is through expanding the call of Galatians 2:20 ("It is not I who live, but Christ who lives in me") as not a choice between life or death, but as the acknowledgement that to follow Christ with radical abandon is both life *and* death; the conjunction is transformed from "but" to "and" ("live *and* die") seeing that to live is to die and to die is what it means to live. As some will discover in reading the chapters that follow, this call will mean setting fire to the need for our identity to be grounded in our own self-sufficiency (the goal of life to care for myself and not need another person) as some *fait accompli*. Additionally, this call will also mean setting fire to the patios of isolation and move more fully to the porch of hospitality by merging and binding our lives to others rather than erecting more arenas of separation. This "releasing call" of the kenotic self that the kenotic turn of Christ provokes for us is ultimately more than laying down some aspect of who we are—it is often setting fire to all that has been and risk becoming something altogether new beyond the event horizon. Perhaps by committing ourselves to this task we can also learn to sing a new song, not one written by the culture *per se*, but the *Carmen Christi* of Philippians 2. Saint Paul offers us a form and depth of life infinitely more profound than much of what is culturally construed as meaningful and deep. As we are challenged by the kenotic call of Christ's life so poetically framed by Paul, we are ultimately called to choose the "form" of faith exhibited by Christ as seen in our cohabitation with others—"getting personal" within the lives of each other as the embodiment of reconciliation, where new communities of meaning can exclaim in one voice, from the porch rather than the patio, that in losing ourselves ("I can't live, with or without you") we have ultimately been found as being something more than we could have hoped for or even imagined. Part of this journey into the life of the kenotic self will entail listening anew to voices that have framed what it means to have cultural identity and discovering how these voices can provide resources for our ever deepening journey of relinquishment. In the next chapter we will look at how two important voices, Aristotle and St. Augustine, speak to the need to develop both external habits of moral living in tandem with a deep understanding of one's interior life.

2

Forming the Kenotic Self, from Aristotle to Augustine

"The whole purpose of places like Starbucks is for people with no decision-making ability whatsoever to make six decisions just to buy one cup of coffee. Short, tall, light, dark, caf, decaf, low fat, non fat, etc. So people who don't know what the hell they're doing or who on earth they are can, for only $2.95, get not just a cup of coffee but an absolutely defining sense of self: Tall. Decaf. Cappuccino."

—Joe Fox in *You've Got Mail*

Is Joe Fox's assessment correct? Is the measure of the "absolutely defining sense of self" in the twenty-first century merely the ability to order whatever coffee style we wish at any given moment, providing the illusion that we are in control of our lives? Do we cover up and accommodate our loss of freedom and control in our fast-paced culture by making mundane choices such as buying coffee infinitely complex in order to mirror the complexity of our very lives—so that if coffee is complex then our lives will become simpler by comparison?

This question of what constitutes the "absolutely defining sense of self" is certainly older than the coffee shop phenomena of the late twentieth century. Consider the following questions:

- What do you value most?

- How do you know that this thing, person, or ideal is the correct thing to value above all else?

- How should you live your life in relation to that thing, person, or ideal that you value so highly above all other things?

In many respects, these three basic questions set the stage for how most people make meaning in their lives before they ever set foot in the doors of a church. For many, it is also the question that haunts their minds as they leave the church on Sunday morning. While the questions may be framed differently given your particular context, the universal concern for "what is of most value" in your life comes through. Two key ways to determine this is a quick assessment of (1) your weekly schedule and (2) what you spent money on in the past week. How we spend our time and money provides a strong (and often painfully authentic!) means of discovering what it is that we truly and deeply "value" above all else. As we begin to recover what it means to be a person committed to the gospel in the world in which we live, we must begin with such an assessment. To be a person of authenticity in the world is to honestly inhabit the crossroads point between what we value most in life and how we act or respond in relation to those things we value most. We have no objective distance in this regard, as the Epistle of James pointedly reminds us—we are what we value and what we do. It is here that we begin to form a sense of identity that is truly *kenotic* rather than fixed, static, and ultimately focused on certainty rather than faith.

Another way we can approach these three questions is through what we see as our core values, morals, and ethics. These three terms can sometimes be seen to mean the same thing. For our purposes, we will define them in the following way:

- *Values*: whatever is of greatest worth and provides the motivation for our morals and ethics

- *Morals*: principles of right and wrong conduct to reinforce and point us toward that which we value; often found in our inner life

- *Ethics*: system of morals and laws by which we seek to realize our highest value; often seen in external codes of conduct

As we begin this journey of attempting to articulate how we form our sense of the kenotic self around the gospel of Jesus Christ, we are thrust headlong in the gathering point of these three: what we value most, how our sense of right and wrong either reinforce or distract us from the highest value in our lives, and what role we play in supporting a system of actions that through collective participation helps realize the kingdom of God on Earth. This gathering point of values, morals, and ethics frame our daily lives in both overt and subtle ways. However, this is not exclusive to those transformed by the Good News. What it means to be a person seeking after what is "good" is a shared concern for Christian and non-Christian alike. In that regard, as tempting as it may be to think that the issue of morality and ethics in relation to who we are as selves in the world is a tangent from what the church has taught regarding how we ground our being, such thinking is deeply false. To be a self emerging into and with Jesus is to fully face the world as an ethically responsible agent. Additionally, to understand the call of the kenotic self, we must additionally understand, embrace, and release that which we value so that we are formed by what we are not as we seek after the face of Christ and not our own understanding.

Let us turn now to two primary ancient sources that have much contemporary relevance for ethics and morality in relation to the formation of identity: Aristotle and St. Augustine. These figures have provided the grounding philosophies for how Western culture understands what it means to be a self and how this understanding is key to our further understanding of ourselves as kenotically motivated and shaped by the *missio Dei*.

ARISTOTLE AND THE GOOD

Aristotle wrote in the late fourth century BCE under very different social and political conditions than characterized the early modern period. In the world of Aristotle, societies existed in realms primarily bounded by the laws of the *civitas* or city-state. The Athenian city-state was not fully realized in Aristotle's life but it was still more than a mere a community of shared values. His was a period of rebuilding, as key leaders had just come through a period in which many had fought and died for conflicting religious beliefs. Central to this rebuilding was how to conceive of a moral order between persons who were deeply divided on matters such as politics, religion, and the nature of family. This is important to remember, as Aristotle writes as though there is a consensus on what matters in life, and as such his philosophy is written to a particular audience of likeminded adherents.

The concept of *morality* as we understand it today plays no apparent role in Aristotle's thought. While the term "moral" appears in translations of Aristotle's text, in such cases it simply carries the meaning of *anything*

26

relating to character in the broadest sense. As such, people are not inherently moral, and our sense of identity is not grounded purposefully in a moral compass. As we will see with Augustine, this internal compass provides an important corrective to Aristotle's philosophy. For Aristotle, the driving question in his grand work on morality—*Nicomachean Ethics*—is, "What is the good, or the chief good?" The modern distinction between *moral* and *non-moral* good plays no role in his thought. He is simply concerned to discover "the good."

Finally, unlike some later philosophers in Western thought, such as Immanuel Kant, Aristotle does not distinguish sharply between science and ethics. For some people today, science is a so-called pure discipline of human discovery, and as such is not inherently a moral or ethical endeavor. Given the role that technology plays in our identity formation in the modern world (think of gaming platforms, social networking, texting, etc.), this synthesis in Aristotle is actually a good one. In that regard, in trying to discover what the good is for human beings, Aristotle is not asking an ethical question as distinct from a scientific question. *According to Aristotle, we do not know the nature of a thing until we know its final cause, what end it tends to realize.* Ethics seeks to discover the good or end of human beings—our final cause, what it is we are really aiming at or are for in life. This would not be a discovery of what we ought to be as opposed to what we are, since according to Aristotle our end is implicit in what we are. In this we are like all natural creatures; to have an Aristotelian nature is to have an end or final cause.

The Key Question for Aristotle: What Is the Chief Good for Human Beings?

Aristotle begins the *Nicomachean Ethics* with the question of *what the chief good is for human beings.* This helps to put focus on how we understand ourselves in and for the world. Until we ask what our purpose is in the world and then live authentically from that place, all our efforts to serve the kingdom of God are built more on effort (what we do) rather than being (who we are). The Psalmist states this question plainly in middle of Psalm 8:

> LORD, our Lord,
> [1] How majestic is your name in all the earth!
> You have set your glory
> above the heavens.

² Through the praise of children and infants
you have established a stronghold against your enemies,
to silence the foe and the avenger.

³ When I consider your heavens,
the work of your fingers,
the moon and stars,
which you have set in place,

⁴ what are mere mortals that you are mindful of them,
human beings that you care for them?

⁵ You have made them a little lower than the heavenly beings
and crowned them with glory and honor.

⁶ You made them rulers over the works of your hands;
you put everything under their feet:

⁷ all flocks and herds,
and the animals of the wild,

⁸ the birds in the sky,
and the fish in the sea,
all that swim the paths of the seas.

⁹ LORD, our Lord,
how majestic is Your name in all the earth![1]

As the Psalmist extols the grandeur of God and the wonder of all creation, all things from the highest heaven to the deepest sea are clearly seen and affirmed. However, there is a vexing question that stands in the midst of creation, as stated in verse 4: "What are mere mortals that you are mindful of them, human beings that you care for them?"

The radical freedom afforded humanity as those members of creation formed in the *imago Dei* moves us into the realm of faith amidst wonder. What is the meaning of being alive? How do we live in relation to all the glory that surrounds us? How do we live in relation to one another in a way that is authentic rather than synthetic?

In keeping with the wide-eyed question of the psalmist, Aristotle poses a similar question for humanity.

Here are two things that are core concerns for Aristotle. First, his question is, what life is best for us (or, rather, best for us humans)? Second, even though he holds that what is intrinsically good about pleasure, wis-

1. TNIV.

dom, and honor is different, nonetheless *there must be a single chief good.*
Why? Because otherwise any conflicts between intrinsic goods would be
irresolvable. Since every action aims at some good, if there is a basis for
choice between "final" goods, it must be some "more final" or "most final"
good. *This is the chief good.*

The Chief Good or Value as Eudaimonia—Joy That Is Flourishing

In his *Nicomachean Ethics*, Aristotle states that, if pressed, all people would
come to some relative agreement that the chief good for which all people
strive is what he terms *eudaimonia*, which can be translated *happiness* but
which might better be understood as *flourishing—living and doing well.*
But beyond that there is not general agreement. *Eudaimonia* is generally
thought to be "most final." Any other final good we may also desire for the
sake of a flourishing life, but such a life we desire only for its own sake.
Therefore it is the most final good. John Stuart Mill, a nineteenth-century
British philosopher and economist, argued that everything else we desire
for its own sake we desire as part of happiness—a point drawn straight
from Aristotle. Additionally, there is a disagreement about what sort of
human life is most flourishing. Some say it is a life of *pleasure*, others of
honor, others a *wealthy life*, others a *virtuous life*. Aristotle understands
that things will break down into these distinctions, but there still remains
a greater calling that is somewhat universal: *to be human is to be motivated by joy that is flourishing.* Additionally, this deep and abiding sense of
joy that is flourishing is not merely a state of mind. Rather, it is something
that gathers all of who we are in body, mind, and soul, and is therefore
only known in *action*. Said another way, the flourishing life of joy is something we *do* as much as who we *are.*

The Role of Virtue in What It Means to Be a Kenotic Self

In book 2 of his *Ethics*, Aristotle goes on to state that the flourishing life
is not merely something sought under the guise of thrill seeking, leisure,
or merely selfish interests. This is the disheartening trend in so many
Christian books seeking to understand Sabbath as merely vacation or
rest for the self apart from work. No, the flourishing life of joy is called
forth by considering and acting as a *virtuous* person actively engaged in
the world. When people think of virtues, we often call to mind idealized
behaviors or noble actions. Think of the great heroes who populate our

collective memory in everything from the epic poetry of Homer's *Odyssey* and *Iliad* to Aragon and Frodo in J. R. R. Tolkien's *Lord of the Rings* to the various superhero archetypes that fill graphic novels, comics, and multiplex movie theaters.

Yet the virtue that Aristotle speaks of is neither the product of being bitten by a radioactive spider like Peter Parker nor solely a product of destiny. Rather, the virtuous life is an art form that is to be practiced. One of the classical Greek terms translated "virtue" is *arete*. For Aristotle, *arete* is the bringing together of that which most exemplifies a person fully alive for the sake of others (*dikaiosyne*; justice) and who yet exhibits *sophrosyne* (self-restraint), or the ability to reflect on their reason for being and therefore act accordingly. In book 2 Aristotle is interested in understanding the nature of *ethical excellences*, those which relate to *passion* and *action*. His general idea is that distinctively human excellence shows itself in the disposition to feel and express passions in certain contexts and in certain ways, and to choose certain kinds of actions for their own sakes. Here are the questions with which Aristotle begins:

- Given that virtues are aspects of "soul," what sort of aspect are they?

- How are virtues acquired?

- What can we learn about what virtues are by considering how they are acquired?

- Given that virtues are human excellences with respect to passions and actions, is there anything general and informative to be said about the kind of relation that exists between virtues and different passions and actions?

We shall address these questions in turn.

Three Things Found in the Soul—Passions, Faculties, and States of Character

In his *Ethics*, Aristotle distinguishes three "things that are found in the soul"—*passions, faculties,* and *states of character*—and gives examples of these. He thinks neither of the former two items can be human excellences, however, because the excellences are that with respect to which we are praised or blamed, and these must "be modes of choice or involve choice." Thus, the virtues are states of character; we are praised or blamed in respect of these. "By states of character [I mean] the things in virtue of which we stand well or badly with reference to the passions, e.g., with reference to anger we stand badly if we feel it violently or too weakly, and well if we feel it moderately; and similarly with reference to the other passions."[2]

Human beings are not simply slaves of passions. We can modulate and mediate our own passions and inform them with a conception of how they are appropriately felt and expressed; doing this appropriately is a distinctively human virtue. *Virtues therefore are acquired by practicing good habits or "habituation"—we become what we do.*

As Aristotle discusses the concern for developing "states of character" within individuals, he settles on the notion of "habit" or "habitation." This, the crux of what it means to develop into a person of virtue in Aristotle, relates to the core concern of this chapter: to develop into a deep and meaningful person presupposes that morals and ethics need to be formed by *external influences*; through right actions and right instruction, individuals will develop into the right kind of people.

As Aristotle muses in the beginning of book 2, "We are not born with them [virtues], nor do we acquire them by any natural process that does not involve our own activity and, perhaps more important, the activity of parents and other elders." This is because "the virtues we get by first exercising them."[3] He goes on to say that "by doing the acts that we do in our transactions with other men we become just or unjust, and by doing the acts that we do in the presence of danger, and by being habituated to feel fear or confidence, we become brave or cowardly. . . . Thus, in one word, states of character arise out of like activities." Said another way, we become virtuous only by doing virtuous acts. In this way, virtue is like having the knack of an art or craft, which we can only acquire by doing. On the other hand, Aristotle claims that "the case of the arts and that of the virtues are not similar." It is not enough that people have the knack, the know-how, or even the habit of doing what the virtuous person does. She must also do them virtuously (excellently)—that is, as the virtuous person would do them. This involves not just what gets done, but what state of character actions realize.

---

2. Aristotle *Ethics* 2.5.

3. Aristotle *Ethics* 2.1.

AUGUSTINE AND THE INNER LIFE OF MORALITY

Turning to the work of St. Augustine of Hippo, who was born centuries after Aristotle in 453 CE yet was still steeped in the predominance of Greek philosophy, we find a very different approach to the question of how we develop morally as individual ethical subjects. As theologian Mark Taylor rightly argues, it is Augustine who first stated the role of the self in the world and "who first recognized and defined the principle of subjectivity."[4] One of the most important works in Western culture is Augustine's autobiographical treatise, *Confessions*. In this masterwork, Augustine attempts to resolve his questions of doubt regarding what it means to be an individual in the world—Who am I? Why am I?—by beginning with the classic question, "How do I know what is right from wrong?" For Augustine, if we can reflect on this question and somehow come to believe in the reality of goodness in our world and that we have some access to this good, then our lives will have some inherent meaning and purpose. As Augustine notes, the interior realm, our inner self, is vastly more complex than the exterior, the world in which we live and move, and is therefore a more likely space to encounter ultimate concerns of meaning and purpose.

The Inner Life Is Filled with Deep and Secret Caverns That Must Be Explored

In book 10 of *Confessions*, Augustine uses the metaphor of the inner life as one of deep "secret caverns." He begins by considering what is "really real" in the world—Does God exist? What is the nature of love? What does it mean to be alive? and so forth—and states that our knowledge is ultimately informed on the one hand by the senses (sight, hearing, touch, taste, smell) while the *true, deep meaning* of this sensory data is only known through retrieval of memory, by reflecting on insights and experiences. As Augustine says, "The answer [to ultimate questions that frame meaning and purpose] must be that they were already in the memory, but so remote and pushed into the background, as if in most secret caverns, that unless they [memories held within the mind] were dug out by someone drawing attention to them, perhaps I could not have thought of them."[5] This is a profound move for Augustine and an important turn in

4. Taylor, *Erring*, 38.

5. Augustine, *Confessions*, 189.

the notion of what constitutes freedom of the self and the journey we take into embracing the possibility found and forged in what we are calling the kenotic self. Another way to say this is that if we were to put Augustine in the Starbucks scenario from *You Got Mail* referred to at the beginning of the chapter, he might argue that long before we stand in line to order a tall decaf cappuccino in the quest for the "absolutely defining sense of self" there resides deep within each of us, tucked away in the secret caverns of the self, the essential building blocks for meaning and purpose in life. In other words, even if you are bedridden, illiterate, or isolated, you have access to the essential building blocks of deep and meaningful life, no less than the world-travelling, highly educated aristocrat does. This speaks volumes to a society that assumes that "knowing oneself" requires accumulating experiences to find the self (more travel, more busyness, and so forth) rather than delving *into* the self we are given, which will give rise to those experiences and ultimately the self God ordains for us.

As philosopher Charles Taylor says of Augustine's move inward, "The world within [our memories, dreams, imagination] proved to be as perplexing as the puzzling world without [what we see, touch, taste and hear]. Rather than a simple individual or singular substance, Augustine found the self to be complex and inwardly divided. . . . It is in a sense the most important one for our spiritual purposes, because the road from the lower to the higher, the crucial shift in direction, passes through our attending to ourselves as inner."[6]

To Be Kenotically Open—You Must Go Inward to Go Outward

One of the more notable quotations by Augustine in this regard is *Noli foras ire, in teipsum redi; in interiore homine habitat veritas* ("Do not go outward; return within yourself. In the inward man dwells truth").[7] Augustine makes this point clear in the following passage:

> What obstacle then remains to hinder the soul from recalling the primal beauty which it abandoned, when it can make an end of its vices? The Wisdom of God extends from end to end with might. By wisdom the great Artificer knit his works together with one glorious end in view. His goodness has no grudging envy against any beauty from the highest to the lowest, for none can have be-

6. Taylor, *Sources of the Self*, 129.

7. Ibid.

ing except him alone. So that no one is utterly cast away from the truth who has in him the slightest vestige of truth. What is it about bodily pleasure that holds us fast? You will find that it is argeeableness. Disagreeable things beget grief and agreeable things beget pleasure. Seek therefore the highest agreeableness. *Do not go abroad. Return within yourself. In the inward man dwells truth*. . . . It [agreeableness] has to do no seeking, but you reach it by seeking, not in space, but by a disposition of mind, so that the inward man may agree with the indwelling truth in a pleasure that is not low and carnal but supremely spiritual.[8]

Augustine is in line with Plato before him in his search for a unifying principle under and throughout the oppositions and complex divisions of the world, and also for how we are to make morally correct decisions based upon upholding the correct values and living them out in proper ethics. But Augustine draws a new direction in his avocation of *in interiore homine* as the *habitat veritas*. As noted by Charles Taylor:

[In] Plato, we find out about this highest principle by looking at the domain of objects which it organizes, that is, the field of the Ideas. What we saw . . . in the image of the eye of the soul was the doctrine that the power of seeing doesn't have to be put into it; rather it just has to be turned. Facing the right field is what is decisive. We may have to struggle to rise to this, but the struggle is over the direction of our gaze. For Augustine, too, God can be known more easily through his created order and in a sense can never be known directly. . . . But our principal route to God is not through the object domain but in ourselves. This is because God is not just the transcendent object or just the principle of order of the nearest objects, which we strain to see. God is also and for us primarily the basic support and underlying principle of our knowing activity. God is not just what we long to see, but what powers the eye which sees. So the light of God is not just "out there," illuminating the order of being, as it is for Plato; it is also an "inner" light.[9]

Given the ultimate and seemingly infinite complexity of this notion of *in interiore homine*, Augustine took the stance that humanity, as fashioned in the *imago Dei* (image of God), sees this *imago Dei* primarily in searching ever deeper into the form of the self, which is the form of God.

8. Augustine, "De vera Religione," 262.
9. Taylor, *Sources of the Self*, 129.

As evidenced in his *Confessions*, Augustine took this path out of his concern to show that God (the ultimate source of meaning for Augustine) is to be found not just in the world we see, touch, taste, and feel but also, more importantly, at the very foundations of our being—we are "hard-wired" to be ethical and moral people. In short, this is what we have been created for.

ARISTOTLE VS. AUGUSTINE—IS OUR SENSE OF SELF SHAPED THROUGH HABITS OR DO WE DRAW TRUTH AND MORALITY FROM WITHIN?

Unlike Aristotle, Augustine does not see "habitation" or developing good habits as the primary means by which we develop into ethical people. Rather, it is by turning *inward—in the interior person dwells truth*—that we discover meaning and find the "moral compass" by which to live; it is the internal life that defines and forms the self. This experience of looking inward rather than developing outward habits results not in self-illumination, but in being illuminated from another source, in receiving the standards of reason and morality from beyond oneself, which his proof for God's existence already brought to light, and which is seen to be very much an experience of inwardness. The more the individual strives to reflect upon itself, the more convinced the subject becomes of the fact that subject and self (knower and known) are one. This truth from both within and from beyond the self brings, for Augustine, the conviction that God stands alongside and not apart from creation in sharing the form of identity and imparting the ability through the "incorporeal light" to judge rightly all things throughout creation and in the realm of imagination.

WHAT DOES ALL THIS MEAN ON A MONDAY MORNING WHEN I HEAD OFF TO WORK?

As you read this, some may wonder why we should spend time studying ethical philosophy when so much of our life requires us to live practically rather than theoretically. Yet as people living in the world we will face ethical dilemmas that are far more perplexing than we ever expected, and we will be called upon to resolve them in ways that give evidence to what we believe based on this key question: What is it you value most? Is the ultimate mark of our humanity the ability to make mundane choices—making a coffee drink complex (tall, decaf, cappuccino)—in order to make our complex world a bit more simplistic in comparison? The answer is a resounding "No!" Rather, to ask along with the Psalmist, "What is humanity that you, oh God, are mindful of us?" (Ps 8:4), is a profound question that deserves full attention and deep reflection. Additionally, we are people who are formed both by the cultural practices that surround us which we use for self-cultivation (Aristotle) and by the inner voice and drive in the depths of our souls (Augustine). Both factors come into play as we develop into the people God has created us to be. It is similar to how stars are formed in the universe: both a great push outward from deep within through millions of atomic reactions, and the powerful push of gravity from surrounding space that forms and shapes the star into a sphere of energy. As Philippians says, we are akin to stars that provide the light of Christ to a dark world. And as stars we too are formed both from deep within and from forces outside ourselves. Like stars, we too are on fire and constantly aglow, casting Christ's light, which is the source of sight to the world around us. To see oneself in this way is to be defined as a kenotic self—not static, always burning, dwelling both in the reality of everyday habits amidst values, morals, and ethics as well as plunging to the infinite depths of one's spirit—a deep that calls out to the deep that is God.

3

The Kenotic Self

Living between Certainty and the Unexpected

But sometimes, very occasionally, songs and books and films and pictures express who you are, perfectly. And they don't do this in words or images, necessarily; the connection is a lot less direct and more complicated than that. . . . It's a process like falling in love. You don't necessarily choose the best person, or the wisest, or the most beautiful; there's something else going on. There is a part of me that would rather have fallen for Updike, or Kerouac, or DeLillo—for someone . . . a little more opaque, and certainly someone who uses more swear words—and, though I have admired those writers, at various stages in my life, admiration is a very different thing from the kind of transference I'm talking about. I'm talking about understanding—or at least feeling like I understand—every artistic decision, every impulse, the soul of both the work and its creator. "This is me," I wanted to say when I read [an important novel]. "I'm not a character, I'm nothing like the author, I haven't had the experiences she writes about. But even so, this is what I feel like, inside. This is what I would sound like, if ever I were to find a voice."[1]

WHAT DOES IT MEAN to find our voice in the world? As author Nick Hornby muses in the quote above, often we find our voice through engaging other voices around us—people we respect, people we admire, and even voices from artistic sources such as paintings, music, novels, movies, and the like. The Victorian poet Matthew Arnold made this point clear in his poem "The Buried Life":

1. Hornby, *31 Songs*, 11.

But often, in the world's most crowded streets,
But often, in the din of strife,
There rises an unspeakable desire
After the knowledge of our buried life;
A thirst to spend our fire and restless force
In tracking out our true, original course;
A longing to inquire
Into the mystery of this heart which beats
So wild, so deep in us—to know
Whence our lives come and where they go.

We live in a time when people struggle to find their voice—to find the depths "into the mystery of this heart which beats / so wild, so deep in us" and the reason for each breath we draw on a cold winter day. Part of that discovery is the realization that the formation of an authentic self that is truly free is more a process than a destination. This is the theme for this chapter; to embrace the path of the kenotic self is to embrace the fact that one is always on a journey to becoming, always navigating the world between moments of seemingly random encounters and divinely inspired epiphanies. Additionally, as will be made clear, a radical and compelling understanding of the kenotic self requires a leap of imagination, which means that fiction (creative arts, novels, poetry, music) can be a good tool for finding a deep sense of self. Bruno Bettelheim, the child psychologist and author of *The Uses of Enchantment*, makes the following observation as to the importance that imagination through fiction (in this case the place fairy tales in the moral development of children) has in the authentic formation of a deep self:

> The child is subject to desperate feelings of loneliness and isola-
> tion, and he often experiences mortal anxiety. More often than not,
> he is unable to express those feelings in words or he can do so only
> by indirection: fear of the dark or of some animal, anxiety about
> his body. Parents tend to overlook . . . those spoken fears. The fairy
> tale, by contrast, takes these existential anxieties and dilemmas
> very seriously and addresses itself directly to them: the need to be
> loved and the fear that one is thought worthless; the love of life,
> and the fear of death. Further, the fairy tale offers solutions in ways
> that the child can grasp on his level of understanding . . . As a child
> listens to a fairy tale, he gets ideas about how he may create order
> out of the chaos that is one's inner life.[2]

2. Bettelheim, *Uses of Enchantment*, 74–75.

Much of what constitutes identity in Western culture is formed and grounded in and through fiction, and this is not necessarily a bad thing. Whether it is through films, music, video games, novels, or the blaring constant assault of viral advertising—we are encouraged as individuals in this culture to engage fictive forms in order to "know thyself." As will be reflected on in the next few pages, the use of imagination in the formation of the self is wonderful and necessary. The challenge before us, however, is a matter of which sources we turn to (or are assaulted by), of how we discern which sources are worthy of being employed, and of the *imago Dei* within each person. In this regard I will turn our attention to the use of art in German Romanticism in what is known as *Bildung*, which is German for "formation." The journey of the kenotic self as one formed through external habits, after Aristotle, and internal convictions and redemption, after Augustine, is similar to how eighteenth-century understandings of the self began—that the self is not only something that becomes, but is also something in need of apprenticeship in becoming. To exemplify this I have chosen to center this reflection primarily on the writings of the German writer Johann Wolfgang von Goethe, in particular his coming-of-age tale of *Wilhelm Meisters Lehrjahre* ("Wilhelm Meister's Apprenticeship"), which is considered to be the forerunner of our modern coming-of-age stories, such as Charlotte Bronte's *Jane Eyre*, J. D. Salinger's *Catcher in the Rye*, and such cinematic tales as the *Star Wars* series and *The Matrix* trilogy. The reason for going back to a somewhat obscure German writer of the Romantic period will hopefully become clear in relation to our postmodern context. As I have written elsewhere, postmodernism, seen by some as a new epoch in thought, is, I argue (at the risk of being flippant), simply German Romanticism with better special effects. Given the questions raised in Romanticism and the amazing similarities in postmodern discourse, Goethe stands out as a notable figure to learn from. Even modern artists such as film director Francis Ford Coppola (*Apocalypse Now*, *The Godfather* trilogy) once commented that "if Goethe were alive today, I think he'd be a filmmaker. His combination of art and science and his enthusiasm for technology is something I recognize in myself."[3] In short, if Goethe has something to say to such a venerable film director, perhaps we should listen!

3. Coppola, 8.

What is core to Goethe's thought is the notion that all of modern life—be it the eighteenth century or the twenty-first—is a reality that is found in the space between representation (*Vorstellung*, what we see and experience in ourselves and in the world) and concept (*Begrifft*, those ideals that animate and drive why and how we love, hate, and despair, and ultimately give rise to *Vorstellung*). These poles of tension, the space between representation and concept, are central to much of Western philosophy and are especially seen in Hegel's *Phenomenology of Spirit*.

In developmental philosophy, George Herbert Mead discussed this tension as the integration of the "I" and "me." For the self to arise, Mead argued, individuals need pragmatic interaction with other people in social settings. In this act of gathering for purposeful interaction (which Mead termed "play") we develop through these social experiences, which are filled with socially symbolic gestures and interactions that get validated by people around us. I hit a homerun in the baseball game, the crowd applauds, and I understand that this action of hitting a homerun is a valued thing and integrate that into my sense of "I" and "me." The "I" is that part of myself (akin to Goethe's *Vorstellung*/representation) that is active and spontaneous, and the "me" (akin to Goethe's *Begrifft*/concept) is the collective responses of others to the "I" that the self internalizes. For example, I may dream of being a guitar player but when I play no one values it or acknowledges it, yet when I play baseball the crowd cheers me on. For Mead, as the "I" and "me" come together, and the gathering point is what we call the "self." This self is often in tension—I want to play guitar, but I also want people to cheer me on, so I continue to play baseball even though I don't really want to.

The polar separation between "I" and "me" is something Goethe is unwilling to resolve and doesn't think can be resolved; there will always be tension between the "I" and the "me." It is this very tension, between representation and what is deep within, that matters in the formation of the self for Goethe. Goethe uses this tension between *Vorstellung* and *Begrifft* as the defining space of the self, and I will argue that it is this tension in part that is the dwelling place of the kenotic self as well. As we will see, Goethe further emphasizes this through his understanding of "morphology," the understanding of the ever-changing nature of the self that he gained from his scientific studies, and his use of the German term *bildung* (formation). Between these poles of representation (what is seen) and concept (what we wish to be), along with the space created between destiny and chance,

Goethe creates a space for locating the kenotic self—in art, theology, and ultimately life itself—which needs to be defined not in static realism but given authenticity in the process of becoming.

In a way, Goethe set a course for Western culture that has largely been overlooked and disregarded in an era that values the immediate and disposable over and against the profound and complex, and relies only that which can be measured *vis-à-vis* the scientific method.[4]

Morphology—the Ever Changing Form of the Self

From his interest in botany, Goethe drew a conception of *morphology* (a phrase which Goethe himself coined) that was a move beyond the rigidity of classification of type[5] toward a conception of *nature as process*. In this regard, such an enterprise as merely *labeling* natural cause and effect was not enough. According to Goethe, what we grasp in labeling are only the *products*, not the *process*, of life. It is the very process of life he wanted to explore, not only as a poet but also as a scientist. Goethe discusses this contrast between static labeling of form and the search for formation in "The Purpose Set Forth" in his work *On Morphology*:

> The Germans have a word for the complex of existence presented by a physical organism: *Gestalt* [structured form]. With this expression they exclude what is changeable and assume that an interrelated whole is identified, defined, and fixed in character. But if we look at all these *Gestalten*, especially the organic ones, we will discover that nothing in them is permanent, nothing is at rest or defined—everything is in a flux of continual motion. That is why German frequently and fittingly makes use of the word *Bildung* [formation] to describe the end product and what is in process of production as well.[6]

In order to see the process, one must look beyond the cataloguing of type in order to gain an appreciation of the whole. In *Naturwiss* he makes the following comment: "Classes, genera, species and individuals are related as instances to a law; they are contained in it, but they do not *contain* or

---

4. Goethe, *Goethe*, 303ff.

5. Goethe had read Linnaeus's system of nature whereby understanding of nature is achieved when "we have succeeded in arranging it (nature) in the pigeonholes of our concepts, dividing it into species and genera, into families, classes, and orders." Ibid.

6. Goethe, "On Morphology," 63.

reveal it."[7] In this regard, Goethe's theory of morphology becomes an able means for reading his coming-of-age work *Wilhelm Meisters Lehrjahre*. To search for systematic stages of development as clearly demarcated sign-posts (class, genus, and species) to show whether a life has moved forward in a systematic paradigm will leave the reader of *Lehrjahre* dismayed. As with his study of nature, Goethe's study of humankind in *Lehrjahre* is not a quantifiable study where the parts equal the whole; instead he offers a portrait through the lives of particular characters that model, rather than explain, the qualities of the realizing self.

Bildung *of Self as Text and Subject / Representation and Concept*

As put by Marc Renfield in *Phantom Formations: Aesthetic Ideology and the Bildungsroman*,

> [Goethe's *Lehrjahre*] narrates the acculturation of a self—the integration of a particular "I" into the general subjectivity of a community, and thus, finally, into the universal subjectivity of humanity . . . even the knowledge of only a dozen words of German suffices to hear an interplay of representation (*Bild*) and formation (*Bildung*) . . . in short, [it] is a trope for the aspirations of aesthetic humanism.[8]

This "interplay" between representation and formation is key to reading *Lehrjahre*, where the distinction between representation (text) and formation (subject) disappears, leaving a new hybrid. In summary, *Lehrjahre* is not a representation of formation, nor is it formation theory placed in an aesthetic casing. As with Goethe's morphology, this is a new "shape" altogether, that while idealized, is nonetheless "real."[9]

---

7. Ibid.; emphasis added.

8. Redfield, *Phantom Formations*, 38.

9. In Goethe's sketch *Gluckliches Ereignis* he reports the following conversation with Schiller regarding his theory of metamorphosis: "We arrived at his house, the conversation began drew me in; there I vigorously expounded the metamorphosis of plants, and with many suggestive strokes of the pen let a symbolic plant arise before his eyes. He listened to and looked at everything with great interest with decided power of comprehension; but when I ended he shook his head and said: 'That is not empirical, that is ideal' (Das ist keine Erfahrung, das ist eine Idee). I was taken aback and somewhat vexed; for he had emphatically stated the point that divided us. . . . But I collected myself and replied: 'I am very glad that I have ideals without knowing it, and even see them with my eyes.'" In Cassier, *Rousseau Kant Goethe*, 73.

Theological Morphology as the Shape of the Kenotic Self

As noted, there is a challenge in deriving a critical reading of *Lehrjahre*, as noted by Redfield in discussing the *Bildungsroman*:

> The *Bildungsroman* paradox derives from that of aesthetics. The "content" of the *Bildungsroman* instantly becomes a question of form, precisely because the content is the forming-of-content, "*Bildung*"—the formation of the human as the producer of itself as form.[10]

Precisely because Wilhelm's *Bildung* in *Lehrjahre* is shown more than explained,[11] the question of content and form regarding the "how" of his *Bildung* can be troubling. Yet a fusion of mind and feeling does progress[12] into the realizing of a portrait of a self who has completed his apprenticeship and is ready for life.[13] For Goethe, the shift must be made from an *empirical* reading of the text to a *morphological* reading in order to see the *Bildung* of Wilhelm take shape—a move that is profoundly theological. In the second portion of Kant's *Critique of Judgment* (*Kritik der Urteilskraft*) entitled "Critique of Teleological Judgment," we see Kant's insights into teleology—the ends giving an understanding of the means—as a heuristic principle for investigation toward understanding. Commenting on the limits of a purely quantified means for understanding of biological nature, he writes,

> It is quite certain that we can never get a sufficient knowledge of organized beings and their inner possibility, much less get an explanation of them, by looking merely to mechanical principles of nature. Indeed, so certain is it, that we may confidently assert that it is absurd for men even to entertain any thought of so doing, or to hope that maybe another Newton may some day arise, to make in-

10. Redfield, *Phantom Formations*, 42.

11. Book 7 of *Lehrjahre* provides an accounting of the "forces" at play in Wilhelm's *Bildung* through the Abbe' and the "unveiling" of the Society of the Tower's apprenticeship. Yet pedagogy is not given beyond "forces at work."

12. As noted by Gerlinde Röder-Bolton, "The concept of *Bildung*, as advocated in *Lehrjahre*, is a fusion of mind and feeling in individuals who respond freely to, and are consciously and inseparably part of, the creative forces of nature. Since this creative power is also within them, prompting them to reshape their inner and outer world, they achieve the full development of their potential." Röder-Bolton, *George Eliot*, 164.

13. As noted in the words of the Abbe' at the conclusion of book 7, "Hail to thee, young man! Thy Apprenticeship is done: Nature has pronounced thee free!" Goethe, *Wilhelm Meister's Apprenticeship*, 2:63.

telligible to us even the genesis of but a blade of grass from natural laws that no design has ordered. Such insight we must absolutely deny mankind.[14]

Even for Kant, a purely mechanistic understanding of living beings was impossible. Destiny and chance seem to go hand in hand as irreconcilable opposites. It was here that Goethe made a connection with Kant's philosophy and gained language for his own theory. In his essay entitled "Einwirkung der neuren Philosophie," from *Naturwiss*, he describes the impact Kant's "Critique of Teleological Judgment" had upon him:

> But the *Critique of Judgment* fell into my hands, and to this book I owe one of the happiest periods of my life. Here I saw my most diverse interests brought together, artistic and natural production handled the same way; the power of aesthetic and teleological judgment mutually illuminated each other. . . . If my way of thinking was not always able to agree with the author's, if I seemed to miss something here and there, still the main ideas of the work were quite analogous to my previous production, action, and thought. The inner life of art as of nature, their mutual working from within outward, were clearly expressed in this book.[15]

In short, for Goethe the process of becoming is to be seen through a veiled morphology rather than a mechanistic system—through an ordering that is organic. Destiny and chance both play a role, neither to the exclusion of the other. In this way, Goethe remembers the heart of theology as the exercise of "formation" rather than "formed," of "becoming" that is the heart of "being."

The Destiny and Chance of Anakin Skywalker

This is similar to the unfolding life narrative of Anakin Skywalker in *Star Wars: Episode 1—The Phantom Menace*. Anakin, whose story unfolds with christological echoes (being born a slave and to a supposed virgin), is embodied fully in his understanding of the world, and his character grows and develops through his encounter with his environment. His training is one of looking into to what "he is destined to be," rather than a systematic shaping of a *tabula rasa*. As Yoda mentions, although he is "the chosen one who will bring balance to the Force," he is one whose "future is

14. Kant, in Cassier, *Rousseau Kant Goethe*, 65.
15. Goethe, in ibid., 64.

clouded." He is to grow into his destiny and be led into it, yet chance is still at work "clouding" this destiny. Anakin is change incarnate, but change with meaning and purpose. As his mother, the Virgin Madonna-esque Shmi Skywalker, muses aphoristically, "You can't stop change any more than you can stop the suns from setting."[16]

In book 1 of Goethe's *Lehrjahre*, Wilhelm is given a similar paradox in the following advice from a stranger he encounters upon the way to an Inn:

> "Do you believe in destiny? No power that rules over us and directs all for our ultimate advantage?"
>
> "The question is not now of my belief; nor is this the place to explain how I may have attempted to form for myself some not impossible conception of things which are incomprehensible to all of us: the question is here: What mode of viewing them will profit us the most? The fabric of our life is formed of necessity and chance; the reason of man takes its station between them, and may rule them both: it treats the necessary as the groundwork of its being; the accidental it can direct and guide and employ for its own purposes; and only while this principle of reason stand firm and inexpugnable does man deserve to be named the god of this lower world. But woe to him who, from his youth, has used himself to search in necessity for something of arbitrary will; to ascribe to chance a sort of reason, which it is a matter of religion to obey!"[17]

As Wilhelm unknowingly begins his apprenticeship, a "stranger" offers this advice to him, as well to the reader of the text. In Wilhelm's approach to life, and the reader's approach to the text, one should not venture to find solace in either the false security of certainty or the supposed freedom offered by chance. Instead, there is a middle way where "the reason of man takes its station *between* [destiny and chance]." Finding this balance will prove hard to maintain, as foreshadowed by Wilhelm in book 2:

> He felt glad as having thus been timefully, though somewhat harshly warned, about the proper path of life; while many are constrained to expiate more heavily, and at a later age, the misconceptions into which their youthful inexperience has betrayed them. For each man commonly defends himself as long as possible from casting out the idols which he worships in his soul, from acknowl-

16. *Star Wars: Episode 1.*

17. Goethe, *Wilhelm Meister's Apprenticeship*, 1:61.

edging a master error, and admitting any truth which brings him to despair.[18]

Wilhelm gains a vision for a life that is free from pedagogical pre-scriptions through his reading of *Hamlet*. Wilhelm states what is key to understanding Prince Hamlet's character:

> It pleases us, it flatters us, to see a hero acting on his own strength, loving and hating as his heart directs him; undertaking and com-pleting; casting every obstacle aside; and at length attaining some great object which he aimed at. Poets and historians would will-ingly persuade us that so proud a lot may fall to man. In *Hamlet* we are taught another lesson: the hero is without a plan, but the piece is a full and rigidly-accomplished scheme of vengeance: a horrid deed occurs; it rolls itself along with all its consequences, dragging guiltless persons also in its course; the perpetrator seems as if he would evade the abyss which is made ready for him; yet he plunges in, at the very point by which he thinks he shall escape and happily complete his course.[19]

Again, Wilhelm relates both instruction and warning to the reader—"the hero is without a plan." There is a destiny, but one without form. To look for a mechanistic means of connecting events in a logical progression via the protagonist's forethought will be to the reader's dismay. Wilhelm, like the plants that helped Goethe gain a concept of morphology, is himself an organic event rather than a static presence. Both the reader and Wilhelm *open* in growth not *through* systematic understanding, but *toward* an end that is the fulfillment of "apprenticeship."

In Wilhelm's reflection on his production of *Hamlet*, he makes this observation:

> In the composition of this play, after the most accurate investiga-tion and the maturest reflection, I distinguish two classes of objects. The first are the grand internal relations of the persons and events, the powerful effects that arise from the characters and proceedings of the main figures: these, I hold, are individually excellent; and the order in which they are presented cannot be improved. No kind of interference must be suffered to destroy them, or even essentially to change their form. These are the things which stamp them-selves deep into the soul; which all men long to see, which no one

18. Ibid., 1:67.
19. Ibid., 1:207.

dares meddle with. Accordingly, I understand, they have almost wholly been retained in all our German theatres. But our country-men have erred, in my opinion, with regard to the second class of objects, which may be observed in this tragedy; I allude to the external relations of the persons, whereby they are brought from place to place, or combined in various ways by certain accidental incidents. These they have looked upon as very unimportant; have spoken of them only in passing, or have left them out altogether. Now, indeed, it must be owned, these threads are slack and slender; and yet run through the entire piece, and bind together much that would otherwise fall asunder, and does actually fall asunder, when you cut them off, and imagine you have done enough and more, if you left the ends hanging.[20]

Wilhelm becomes aware that an understanding of one's *Bildung* is found in the space between these poles, the first being "the grand internal rela-tions of the persons and events, the powerful effects which arise from the characters and proceedings of the main figures."[21] This is an accounting of the obvious—that which is not only seen by the self, but is also evidenced by others. Yet there is a second class of objects that also plays a role in one's *Bildung*, those being "the external relations of the persons, whereby they are brought from place to place, or combined in various ways by certain accidental incidents."[22] *In short, the kenotic self is located between what is seen and what is not seen; between the represented self and the conceptual self exists the authentic kenotic self.*

Goethe's Slender Threads and Shuffling Baudrillard in The Matrix

This tension between the represented self and the conceptual self is portrayed vividly in *The Matrix*. In the beginning of the film, Thomas Anderson, the protagonist, whose true name is Neo[23] (played by Keanu Reeves), goes to a secret hiding place in his apartment that holds a copy of

20. Ibid., 1:241.

21. Ibid.

22. Ibid.

23. As stated by Agent Smith in *The Matrix*, "It seems that you've been living two lives. In one life, you're Thomas A. Anderson, program writer for a respectable software company. You have a Social Security number, you pay your taxes, and you help your landlady carry out her garbage. The other life is lived in computers, where you go by the hacker alias 'Neo' and are guilty of virtually every computer crime we have a law for. One of these lives has a future, and one of them does not." *The Matrix*.

Baudrillard's *Simulacra and Simulation*. He turns to the chapter entitled "On Nihilism." The book is merely a shell—a metaphor for the hollowness of so-called reality—that holds a computer disc. This use of Baudrillard is by no means accidental. For readers of Jean Baudrillard, it is worth noting that "On Nihilism" is not actually located in the middle of *Simulacra and Simulation* as shown in *The Matrix*—the chapter actually closes the book. As noted by Jim Rovira,

> this misplacement of the chapter serves as a device employed by the film makers to provide specific philosophical context for this complicated, intriguing film. While such widely divergent streams such as Christ imagery, eastern philosophy, and Greek mythology all inform the narrative and the characters, Baudrillard's *Simulacra and Simulation* is probably the best starting point for a philosophical and sociological approach to the movie's content.[24]

Baudrillard borrows from Ecclesiastes in *Simulacra and Simulation* when he asserts that "the simulacrum is never that which conceals the truth—it is the truth which conceals that there is none. The simulacrum is true."[25] In *The Matrix*, the reality of earth as we know it is gone. The "real" world is a "desert of the real," in the words of Morpheus—a nuclear wasteland is all that remains and humanity exists in a simulacrum of reality as we need it to be: jobs, shopping, skyscrapers, and so forth provided by AI so we will be content. According to Baudrillard, the truth pulled over our eyes is that "the simulation is infinitely more dangerous since it always suggests, over and above its object, that law and order themselves might really be nothing more than a simulation."[26]

As with Baudrillard's "simulation," so also Goethe's poetics preserves a space between destiny and chance, between concept and representation, that opens a gap of the possible that is without truth yet is the truth. Baudrillard asserts that the simulacrum is never that which conceals the truth; rather it is the "truth" that conceals that there is no so-called truth. Goethe in his "morphological poetics" leaves the reader and the protagonist of the fiction "without a plan" and with the troubling reality that what you see (and read) is all that you will get. There is no "destiny," yet at the same there is no "chance" in Goethe's universe. Paradoxically, one's life can-

24. Rovira, "Baudrillard and Hollywood."

25. Baudrillard, "Simulacra and Simulation," 166.

26. Ibid., 177.

not be planned, yet one must plan a life. There are "accidental incidents" that arise and give shape to one's identity. These are not to be discounted nor dismissed, as Wilhelm's contemporaries have erred to do. Throughout *Lehrjahre*, characters continually appear seemingly "by chance" and offer necessary information and direction for Wilhelm as if by mystical means. This comes to its most grandiose point with the revealing of Wilhelm's "apprenticeship" in book 7 by the Abbe' and the Society of the Tower. As it is revealed to Wilhelm that his "life" has been guided, he is told the following:

> "Perhaps," continued his interrogator, "we should now be less at variance in regard to Destiny and Character."
>
> Wilhelm was about to answer, when the curtain quickly flew together. "Strange!" said Wilhelm to himself: "Can chance occurrences have a connection? Is what we call Destiny but Chance?"[27]

Here Wilhelm echoes the advice of the "stranger" in book 1, quoted earlier, where he is advised that

> the fabric of our life is formed of necessity and chance; the reason of man takes its station between them, and may rule them both: it treats the necessary as the groundwork of its being; the accidental it can direct and guide and employ for its own purposes; and only while this principle of reason stand firm and inexpugnable does man deserve to be named the god of this lower world.[28]

In order to return to this truth, however, Wilhelm's "apprenticeship" is rendered descriptively rather than prescriptively. He, like the reader, must discover that the "end" is not necessarily easy to discern in an orderly manner. The "threads of life" are indeed slack and slender. They run through the entire piece and "bind together much that would otherwise fall asunder."[29] It is this action of bringing together that the self is known, not in the threads of destiny and chance, representation and concept. It is in the working of slack and slender realities that the weaving of a self is actualized—not in the threads, but in the pattern itself. To paraphrase the words of Trinity to Neo in *The Matrix*, the "Matrix" of the threads can't tell

---

27. Goethe, *Wilhelm Meister's Apprenticeship*, 60.

28. Ibid., 61.

29. Ibid., 241.

you who you are.[30] In short, we begin where we are, and it is *process*, not production, that is all there is.

However, this is not the proverbial end of the story, nor a reason for lament. The hope we can gain from embracing the true self as one that is in process rather than merely produced in a functional intent is a return theologically to a very important concept—*sanctification*. Core to the Christian story is a call of the self that goes beyond mere justification—being made right and atoned (at-oned) with the Living God. This justification begets a life—a new birth—that is entwined into eternally deepening and ever-expanding encounters with God in accord with service to and with God's kingdom. As we live into the world as the kenotic self, we are ever changing and deepening our life in and through the life of God in Christ. It is this life that is radically compelling to a bored and burned-out generation tired of mere platitudes and empty doctrine. To continually live out our lives in deeper and deeper sanctification, to strive into a holy and ever-enlivening presence of the holy that will never be exhausted—this is a life worthy of the *imago Dei* within us and of the God for whom the depths of the kenotic self cry out.

30. Trinity also makes this rather Goethe-esque statement at the beginning of *The Matrix*: "The answer is out there, Neo. It's looking for you. And it will find you if you want it to."

4

Grounding the Kenotic Self through the Mission of God amidst a Cultured World

> This [current generation is immersed in a] relentless cult of nov-
> elty, with its assertion that art need not be good or pure, just so
> long as it is new, newer, and newer still, conceals an unyielding
> and long-sustained attempt to undermine, ridicule and uproot all
> moral precepts. There is no God, there is no truth, the universe is
> chaotic, all is relative, "the world as text," a text any postmodern-
> ist is willing to compose. How clamorous it all is, but also—how
> helpless.[1]

NOBEL LAUREATE ALEKSANDR SOLZHENITSYN, upon winning the
National Arts Club Medal of Honor for literature, made the above
comment in his acceptance speech, assessing the dawn of the twenty-first
century. Is Solzhenitsyn correct? Is this merely a generation immersed in
a relentless cult of novelty, or is there hope?

As we find the kenotic self formed both from within (Augustine)
and from habits lived outside of ourselves (Aristotle), and ultimately lived
into the world as a narrative formed and figured—emerging—amidst
certainty and the unexpected (Goethe), for what purpose does this self
continue to be grown and shaped? Or, to pose the same question in line
with Rick Warren, what is the "purpose" in a purpose-driven life?[2] As I
mentioned at the beginning of this book, the kenotic self is one formed
not merely for itself, but onto-missionally, that is, being-as-mission. More
specifically, the kenotic self is one who is profoundly called (*vocare*) into
the world through and with the *missio Dei*.

---

1. Solzhenitsyn, "Relentless Cult," 17.
2. See Warren, *Purpose Driven Life*.

What Is This Mission and How Does the Self Realize Itself through It?

To begin our discussion, consider the following two key statements with regard to mission. First, from Darrell Guder in *Missional Church: A Vision for the Church in North America*, "The basic function of all theology is to equip the church for its calling. If that calling is fundamentally missional, then what we understand and teach about the church will shape and serve to equip people to be faithful witness in particular and unique places."[3] Second is Johannes Verkuyl's operational definition of missiology in *Contemporary Missiology*: "Missiology is the study of the salvation activities of the Father, Son, and Holy Spirit throughout the world geared toward bringing the Kingdom of God into existence. Missiology's task in every age is to investigate scientifically and critically, the presuppositions, motives, structures, methods, patterns of cooperation, and leadership which the churches bring to their mandate."[4] Take a moment and reflect on these two definitions of what constitutes mission as we reflect on the role it plays in the grounding of the kenotic self.

How Do These Statements Confirm, Challenge, or Even Perplex Your Understanding of What the Church Is Called to in the World?

What the church has understood to be missiology has, for most of the last two millennia, often been a singular and at times rhetorical pronouncement uttered from the church to the world it has sought to save unilaterally. This "Great Commission" drive of the church as a going-out activity has a dark side: it can presuppose an essential grounding or loci of concern whereby revelation and commissioning for mission rarely occurs. At the beginning of the nineteenth century, as Western missionaries took the gospel to the ends of the earth, the church began to take root in non-Western lands in record numbers. However, all too often, both the text of Jesus Christ (the *Logos*) and the context of Western culture (the *ethnos*) were transmitted to new peoples without any distinction. We witness the consequences of that approach today.

Because the view of both Western and non-Western Christians is largely that of the Euro-American theological construct to first be "correct" in their theology prior to their practice of piety which gives rise to deep theology, non-Western churches unwittingly mimic the Western

3. Guder, *Missional Church*, 12.

4. Verkuyl, *Contemporary Missiology*, 5.

Christian communities shaped by Western thought and practices. There seems to be little awareness that what has come to be known as systematic theology by much of the academy is ultimately a Western contextual theology. As David Bosch points out, "Our entire context comes into play when we interpret a biblical text. One therefore has to concede that all theology . . . is, by its very nature, contextual."[5] This observation makes no judgment as to the rightness or wrongness of the theology itself; only that "systematic" describes an approach that fits particularly well with Greek philosophy and Enlightenment rationalism. In the thirteenth century, Thomas Aquinas called his magisterial treatise, a synthesis of Aristotelian logic and Christian theology, the *Summa Theologiae* or "sum of theology." In similar fashion, much of theological scholarship in the twentieth and early twenty-first century has prioritized the systematic as the form by which authoritative renderings of core doctrine and piety are to be measured and, by association, relegated contextual theologies to the periphery, if they are recognized at all. This dominance of theological form over and against other contextually cultural forms of rendering the gospel is an issue that needs to be considered particularly within Evangelicalism. In his book *The Next Reformation: Why Evangelicals Must Embrace Postmodernity*, Carl Raschke notes that evangelicalism has "adopted by its own means and measure the criteria of conceptual adequacy that were put forth centuries ago by modern philosophy, it has ingested that unique fashion of idolatry."[6] Raschke references Bruce Ellis Benson's book *Graven Ideologies: Nietzsche, Derrida, and Marion on Modern Idolatry*, and states that this modernist idolatry embraced by Evangelicalism can be seen in three ways: (1) a critical stress on the autonomy of the individual, (2) a strong confidence in the powers of human reason in general and the rationality of the individual, and (3) the pure "objective" character of reason itself.[7] When we refer back to the *Carmen Christi* text of Philippians 2 addressed in the first chapter, what we see is a different emphasis—an emphasis that points not to reason but to vocation or calling.

In his inaugural lecture at Princeton Seminary, Darrell Guder made the assertion that missional theology is that sphere of Christian reflective

---

5. Bosch, *Transforming Mission*, 423.

6. Raschke, *Next Reformation*, 23.

7. Ibid.

action that is bound up in a deep and abiding call first and foremost and often beyond reason. This focus is

> derived from the church's missional vocation. That vocation is the will and command of the church's Lord, and the formation of this community for its missional vocation is the work of the Spirit promised and sent by the Lord of Church. This is the common and pervasive message of the apostolic *kerygma* and its scriptural record. You shall be my witnesses; as my Father has sent me, so I send you; Go into all the world and disciple the nations; you are "chosen race, a royal priesthood, a holy nation, a people for God's own possession, so that [it] may proclaim the excellencies of Him who has called it out of darkness into His marvelous light" (1 Peter 2:9). When mission accompanies theology, when it defines the way theology works, then it becomes the task of such missional theology to accompany and support the church in its witness by testing all that the church says and does in terms of its calling to be Christ's witness.[8]

Guder supports this field of study as authentic to the Christian self-understanding *vis-à-vis* Karl Barth's challenge in regards to the "obligation" that theology *qua* theology has to the "witness of its word":

> There would be no theology if there were not a community obligated in a special way to the witness of its word. Its central problem is posed for theology not in an empty space but by the community's ministry, and this is the problem that constitutes theology as a science next to other sciences. If one disregards its origin in the ministry of the community, then all of its problems would lose their theological character, if they had not become ephemeral already, and they would be consigned to the area of general and especially historical arts and letters. . . . In the ministry of theology, the community tests all that it does on the basis of the criterion given by its commission, ultimately and finally in the light of the word of its Lord and Commissioner.[9]

What is the missional context within which the *missio Dei* resides today in Western culture? Given the role social sciences have played in the formation of cultural identity in the late twentieth and early twenty-first centuries, it is helpful to look toward the social sciences aligned with missional theology in order to better assess the current state of Western

8. Guder, "From Mission and Theology."
9. Karl Barth, *Kirchliche Dogmatik* IV/3, quoted in ibid., 46.

culture in regards to beliefs and practices. For example, the Survey of Political Culture at the University of Virginia included a study of Western European core commitments and found that people generally fit into six categories depending on their commitment to self vs. others, truth vs. relativism, and traditional moral codes vs. personally established codes. The results were as follows:

Traditionalists	11 %
Neo-traditionalists	16 %
Conventionalists	15 %
Pragmatists	14 %
Communitarians	19 %
Permissivists	27 %

It should not come as a shock that the dominant category of commitment is one of *permissiveness*, defined as the most lenient in attitude toward traditional morality, the most relativistic in worldview, and the most hedonistic when it comes to weighing between one's sense of self-interest and the common good. Does a missional theology speak to those who see permissiveness as one of the highest cultural values?

While permissiveness is a high value in Western culture today, this should not lead us to think that this is also a culture where people are indifferent to spiritual matters. In the periodical *Re:Generation*, John Seel, of the Post-Modernity Project at the University of Virginia, wrote an intriguing article entitled "Meet Your Neighborhood Neo-pagan" stating that people are indeed deeply concerned about spirituality, but perhaps in ways we may not expect. In his article Seel argues that while the American experiment for the past two hundred years has desired to view itself as a "Christian nation"—a designation made popular recently by writer Sam Harris's polemical attack on evangelicalism in his book *Letter to a Christian Nation*—this view needs to be reevaluated beyond mere politics and heritage. "With its moral compass adrift," Seel writes, "and its cultural North Star no longer fixed upon Puritan or Enlightenment foundations, America seems to be searching for something spiritual it can sink its teeth into."[10] Part of the push is to acknowledge that reason alone and tradition

---

10. Seel, "Meet Your Neighborhood Neo-pagan," 18.

alone are not enough for most people. There is an evident hunger after the "buried life" according to Seel's study and findings.

As we sit in the smoldering wreckage of modernity, that project handed down by such thinkers as Immanuel Kant and Adam Smith that told us that everyone is indeed an individual, an "island adrift from the continent," we need a return to what W. B. Yeats termed our "true original face." For some, this has been the embrace of the neo-pagan.

From Postmodern to Neo-pagan

Many continue to argue that the dominant worldview in Western culture is predominately postmodernity (a term that is so over-used that, in a recent article from the *Chronicle of Higher Education*, one writer said that the term had the effectiveness today of an old kitchen sponge—it had its day and now needs to be discarded). Yet while academics, journalists, fiction writers, and college workers discuss and dissect the postmodern implications of this and that, Western culture has gone for something much more profound—neo-paganism. Tenets of neo-paganism include the following:

1. A rejection of the consequences of modernity: secularization, disenchantment, and rationalization.

2. A quest to "resacralize one's world—to restore a sense of mystery after the disenchantment of modernity." In the words of writer Norman Lear, "We have become a numbers-oriented culture that puts more faith in what we see, touch, and hear, and is suspicious of the unquantifiable, the intuitive, the mysterious."[11] Neo-paganism is a quest for spirituality without a grounded spirit or sense of authority outside of oneself.

3. A loose description of modern variations on ancient beliefs from pre-Christian mystery religions. Margot Adler, a reporter on National Public Radio and a self proclaimed Wicca witch, has described neo-paganism as a worldview that holds that "the world is holy. Nature is holy. The body is holy. Sexuality is holy. The mind is holy. The imagination is holy. You are holy. A spiritual path that is not stagnant ultimately leads one to the understanding of one's own divine nature.

---

11. Lear, quoted in Seel, 18.

Thou art Goddess. Thou art God. Divinity is imminent in all Nature. It is as much within you as without."[12]

In the *Re: Generation* article mentioned earlier, John Seel outlines six additional elements of common to neo-paganism that are helpful channel markers:

- *Animism*: "the view that Nature (always capitalized) is sacred and all things are imbued with a certain vitality, 'divine spark,' or life force. "It (the Force) is all around us" taught Master Yoda to his lone disciple Luke Skywalker. 'Life creates it. We are luminous beings, not this crude matter you feel.'"

- *Pantheism*: "the view that divinity is inseparable from Nature and is imminent in Nature: the world is all that is, and since experience tells us how small a part of this totality we are, we draw the conclusion that we are playthings of hidden forces. . . . Pagan wisdom consists in the attempt to understand this life and to properly place human beings in the order of powers."

- *Polytheism*: "the view that reality is multiple and diverse. In Neo-paganism there is 'radical inclusively' that is in direct contrast to the exclusivity of orthodox Christianity, Judaism, and Islam. In *Drawing Down the Moon*, Margot Adler makes the statement that 'Monotheism is but imperialism in mission.'"[13]

- *Subjectivity*: "the view that spirituality is to be based on your own subjective experience and personal vision rather than objective dogma or written creeds."

- *Reintegration*: "the view that the goal of spirituality is to relink or reconnect the self with Nature. There is a strong element of 'holism' in Neo-paganism—everything is related. 'Neopaganism is the return to the ancient idea' states Adler, 'that there is no distinction between spiritual and material, sacred and secular.'"[14]

- *Self-Divination*: "the view that autonomy is spirituality." "Despite all the evidence," states Seel, "a good case can be made for the proposition that what attracts members of a weakened Christian civilization

12. Adler, quoted in Seel, 19.
13. Adler, quoted in Seel, 21.
14. Ibid.

to Oriental creeds and occult doctrines is not Buddhism, the Tantra, the Tao, Zen, Brahmanism, or shamanism. Much more important, it seems to me, is the presence in each of these new missions of the pantheistic world view and the hope of self-divination, or at least self-elevation above the status of mere creature."[15]

How Does a Neo-pagan Worldview Shape How the Kenotic Self Develops?

The assertion that the culture that forms and infuses the development of the kenotic self is more evidenced by neo-paganism rather than post-modern categories is vital for a number of reasons. As seen in the beginning chapters of this book, the kenotic self is formed both internally and externally—by the culture that surrounds us as well as the *imago Dei* within us. If we acknowledge that the culture around us is not indifferent or wholly ignorant to spiritual matters, then we will seek different categories and language with which to understand ourselves and our culture. While the world that surrounds us is certainly not entirely Christian, it is also not entirely secular either. British poet and priest Gerard Manley Hopkins states it well in his poem "God's Grandeur":

> The world is charged with the grandeur of God.
>   It will flame out, like shining from shook foil;
>   It gathers to a greatness, like the ooze of oil
> Crushed. Why do men then now not reck his rod?
> Generations have trod, have trod, have trod;
>   And all is seared with trade; bleared, smeared with toil;
>   And wears man's smudge and shares man's smell: the soil
> Is bare now, nor can foot feel, being shod.
>
> And for all this, nature is never spent;
>   There lives the dearest freshness deep down things;
> And though the last lights off the black West went
>   Oh, morning, at the brown brink eastward, springs—
> Because the Holy Ghost over the bent
>   World broods with warm breast and with ah! bright wings.

As Hopkins notes, the world and all that is in it is nourished and sustained by the power and presence of God as a mother nourishes her child through her very body. God is in no way distant or removed from our

---

15. Seel, "Meet Your Neighborhood Neo-pagan," 19.

lives—even the lives of those indifferent or ignorant to this nourishing presence. This leads to my next point: that what constitutes discussions surrounding postmodern theory is rhetoric concerned primarily with the mind rather than our whole selves. Granted, postmodern theorists such as Michel Foucault, Jacques Derrida, and Luce Irigaray among others share a concern for the body and sociological reform, but the language categories by which dialogue occurs in much of what people consider "postmodernity" is a philosophical post-Enlightenment concern that puts embodiment aside as a secondary issue (as we look to the Continental philosophers in later chapters, we will address thinkers who both acknowledge a post-Enlightenment critique yet offer helpful pragmatics for living, and not merely disembodied theory). As such the church, in its dialogues that surround postmodernity, begins and ends discussions in purely theoretical and ultimately disembodied categories—rarely touching the ground beneath our feet. In these ways, moving the postmodern issue aside in favor of the neo-pagan creates a more embodied, more holistic place to dialogue with the culture around us—a culture not separate from a life of the spiritual or indifferent to it. As the kenotic self develops and grows in a neo-pagan world, we are alerted to some provocative challenges in relation to how we articulate what we see as truth.

First, a neo-pagan context teaches us that truth is articulated through a primarily aesthetic, embodied medium over and against disembodied propositional rhetoric.

Some of this can be seen in the way the purchasing of books is at an all-time high while cultural literacy is continuing to drop. Consider the fact that while reading is at an all-time low in America, sales at mega stores such as Borders and Barnes & Noble is rising. Why? One argument is that the *aesthetic* of having books is still valued, although the reading of them is not. Mark Twain's quote that "a room without books is a body without a soul" speaks to the cultural value of the presence of books, although actually learning from them is not valued. That said, people are not indifferent to truth claims—that which is meaningful, rich with beauty, and compelling amidst pain and loss still holds sway with humanity. However, the categories and means by which people will engage meaningful dialogue has changed dramatically. In this way the kenotic self often seeks symbols and images that go beyond language systems—think of the rise of YouTube as a visual medium—over and against mere argumentation.

Secondly, the rise of neo-paganism as the context in which cultural iden-
tity is formed means that individuals are indeed allowing for mystery and
paradox in their lives amidst relationships. The days of "Evidence demands
a verdict" alone are waning.

In this point we need to remember that in a neo-pagan context cultural identity is formed for individuals through continual dialogue about
truth that gathers around shared images verses ascribed creeds. People
will draw close to compelling filmic narratives and create space for possibility and expand horizons. More and more people discuss television
shows and films than they do propositional truth claims as isolated activities of the mind. My undergraduate students will spend hours watching
entire seasons of a television show on DVD and then flawlessly quote line
after line to each other. When they approach the creeds and confessions
of the church, they will affirm the doctrinal depth and veracity of them,
but these profoundly deep statements rarely enter into their day-to-day
dialogue and life. Part of this is due to the fact that filmic presentations are
always formed with a narrative—a story that is relatable to our common
human experience. As much as people will argue that we have lost the
hunger for metanarrative—a binding story that gives meaning and depth
to our lives—the evidence around us is to the contrary. People hunger and
thirst for compelling narratives that do not seek to provide easy answers
and expand rather than restrict the horizon of the human condition. This
is a point that neo-paganism asserts that Western culture, with its high
valuation of film, concurs with. This is where the church needs to embrace the fact that people are looking for a compelling metanarrative to
give meaning to their particular life narrative. In short, the question is
not whether the kenotic self will accept a metanarrative to ground its life
upon, but which narrative it is currently living through and why.

Another indicator of this hunger for narrative is seen in the growing
video game industry. As more and more relational growth occurs in the
virtual realm, there will be an ever-increasing need for opportunities to
experience relational growth, emotional joys and disappointments, which
will be framed by narrative and the formation of the self. MIT professor
Sherry Turkle, in her book *Life on the Screen: Identity in the Age of the*
Internet, makes the following point: "[O]nce we take virtuality seriously
as a way of life, we need a new language for talking about the simplest
things. Each individual must ask: What is the nature of my relationships?
What are the limits of my responsibility? And even more basic: Who

and what am I?" [16] The virtual realm provides a level of personal reflection and growth that ultimately (1) cannot be sustained in real life and (2) will hamper growth and intimacy. This virtual development of identity contains more of the unbridled idealism of Nietzsche and Schopenhauer than a grounded identity in the person of Christ. Consider the advertisement for the game Obsidian:

> Obsidian. Your rules don't apply here. You arrive, a stranger in a strange land. Confused, disoriented, you make way through the twisted, surreal world in search of your partner, Max. All you carry with you is the knowledge you've grown to accept as the truth. But you're about to discover that what the truth is depends on what world you're in. And in this world, things don't necessarily work the way you might expect them to. The characters don't exactly act the way they're supposed to. The laws of physics have somehow become warped. What is up and what is down is merely a matter of opinion.

Finally, to understand the cultural formation of the kenotic self in today's neo-pagan culture is to understand that what it means to be human in the twenty-first century is ultimately some extension of the organic body as post-human.

The term "post-human" can conjure images of Gothic science fiction akin to Mary Shelley's *Frankenstein*. The question of posthumanism is ultimately the question of what constitutes our essential identity—is what it means to be human only organic and biological? Steven Pinker, a cognitive neurosurgeon, in his book *How the Mind Works*, asks this question in reference to the paradox posed by the first century Greek historian Plutarch regarding what is called the "ship of Theseus." As history records, the ship on which the warrior Theseus and the youth of Athens returned

16. Turkle, *Life on the Screen*, 15. Turkle makes the observations that with networked computers, people are creating alternative identities, forming disembodied relationships, and building imaginary places that are beginning to interest and involve us as much as those in the physical world. As youth spend more time in the Mac and Windows operating system interfaces—which allow us to run several applications at once, cycling among different work and play identities throughout the day—this encourages them to think of our minds and selves as multiple and decentralized. Turkle surmises her comments by stating that rather than a luddite repose to technology, these changes can have positive effects, but only if we are willing to accept that they are already happening and be thoughtful in deciding what we wish to do with them. We must be aware of how computer-mediated relationships work if we want to optimize the human side of the relationship.

after defeating Crete had thirty oars, and was preserved by the Athenians down even to the time of Demetrius Phalereus, for they took away the old planks as they decayed, putting in newer and stronger timber in their place. As Plutarch ponders, this ship became a standing example among the Stoic philosophers for whether something over time is ever still the "same thing" if it is subsequently replaced, even subtly, to the point that nothing original remains. As Pinker reframes the story in light of medical advances, he proposes the following "ship of Theseus" paradox for the post-human:

> Surgeons replace one of your neurons with a microchip that duplicates its input-output functions. You feel and behave exactly as before. Then they replace a second one, and a third one, and so on, until more and more of your brain becomes silicon. Since each microchip does exactly what the neuron did, your behavior and memory never change. Do you even notice the difference? Does it feel like dying? Is some other conscious entity moving in with you?[17]

As we continue to augment the human organism—whether it is subtle as in education about philosophy and theology (an argument against innateism), or the biochemical augmenting of our moods (Lithium and Prozac), or birth control, or the biological replacement of vital organs (artificial hearts, lungs, kidneys)—what remains truly human?

As alluded to in the previous section, this extends into the realm of identity at a psychological and spiritual level with the formation and maintenance of identity in the virtual realm. This synthesis of the spiritual and cybernetic is celebrated by some people as "cyberpunk," a late twentieth-century hybrid term that fuses "cybernetics" (the science of communication and control theory) and "punk" (the branding of alternative, antisocial rebels). Writer Bruce Sterling has called this subcultural shift "an unholy alliance of the technical world with the underground of pop culture and street-level anarchy . . . a place where the worlds of science and art overlap, the intersection of the future and the now . . . the fusion of the human and the machine at last."[18] Phillip Elmer-DeWitt in 1993 launched *Time Online*, the online e-zine of Time-Warner. In an article

17. Pinker, *How the Mind Works*, 146.

18. Sterling, *Mirrorshades*, xii.

entitled "Cyberpunk!" Elmer-Dewitt outlined the following values of the cyber-obsessed:

> Information wants to be free: A good piece of information-age technology will eventually get into the hands of those who can use it to its fullest potential, despite the oppression of copyright laws, censors, and "datacops."[19]

As noted by Elmer-Dewitt, there is a radical desire for freedom in the cyberpunk culture. The belief they can run the world for the better if they can only get their hands on the control box is a core value. He who has the faster broadband will win the day. Other core values include:

- *Promote decentralization*: Society is splintering into hundreds of sub-cultures and designer cults, each with its own language, code, and life-style.

- *Surf the edges*: When the world is changing by the nanosecond, the best way to keep your head above water is to stay at the front end of the Zeitgeist.

- *Life is data*: Cyberpunk Christopher Myers is quoted by Elmer-DeWitt as saying, "History is a funny thing for cyberpunks . . . it's all data. It all takes up the same amount of space on disk, and a lot of it is just plain noise."[20]

As Elmer-Dewitt surmises in his article,

> Cyberspace is a real place. We all have addresses there, experience traffic jams, lose our temper and get embarrassed and amazed by what happens before our eyes (and if you have a decent sound card . . . our ears). While we may merely "dabble" on the Internet, some of our students live there more fully than anywhere else. Proof of this occurred in 1991 when The WELL, one of the most unified cybercommunities on the Net, had a tragedy occur. One of its most active members ran a program that erased every message he had ever left—thousands of postings, some running for pages. It was an act that amounted to virtual suicide. A few weeks later, he committed suicide for real.[21]

19. Elmer-DeWitt, "Cyberpunk!"
20. Ibid.
21. Ibid.

A Look at the Emergent Church Response to Western Culture

As mentioned, one model that is currently providing an attempt at integrating both the classic missional priorities of the church with the neo-pagan and cyberpunk culture of twenty-first century Western culture is what is termed the "Emerging church." What has "emerged" in this movement, through the prolific writings of Brian McLaren, Dan Kimbell, Leonard Sweet, and others, is a form of what I term "neo-correlational theology"— which has particular roots in the work of University of Chicago theologians Paul Tillich and Don Browning. This Emergent movement draws some strength from a renewed interest in Tillich's systematic and methodological presentation of what he termed a "theology of culture," first presented in his 1919 address *Über die Idee einer Theologie der Kultur* ("On the Idea of a Theology of Culture"). While not directly appealing to Tillich's influential insights and legacy, Emergent discussions surrounding what it deems vital for the church's authentic mission are Tillich's legacy through and through.

As some of these more broad descriptions certainly show, the Emergent church movement aligns itself with what Tillich alluded to in his prolific writing. The Emergent movement frames with Tillich in numerous ways, but most clearly n the meta-question of religious form in relation to content and meaning. As Tillich makes clear in "On the Idea of a Theology of Culture," religion is not conceived as one cultural function among many. Rather, religion is the directedness toward the unconditional depth of meaning in each of these cultural functions. Tillich writes that "[t]hrough existing realities, through values, through personal life, the meaning of unconditional reality becomes evident . . . before which personality and community are shattered in their own self-sufficient being and value." The unconditioned depth of cultural functions is "not a new reality, alongside or above other things." It is not a being, nor the substance or totality of beings; "it is—to use a mystical formula—that which is above all beings which at the same time is the absolute Nothing and the absolute Something."[22] This turn to the existential, mystical, and apophatic in Tillich's "Theology of Culture" is core to the Emergent church move toward the "organic vintage-faith approach" to mission for the "post–seeker-sensitive," which is grounded in the nonfoundational. Critiquing what he terms the "modern linear approach" to mission, which has everything

22. Tillich, "On the Idea," 165.

planned and focused on "the message as the focal point and centerpiece of the service," Dan Kimbell in his book *The Emerging Church* states that the "organic vintage-faith approach" provides a form of mission as "gathering" that highlights "the experiential . . . [that] is woven into and flows throughout the gathering as the focal point and centerpiece."[23]

The Emergent church methodology of cultural engagement in and through mission is drawn from the dialectic methodology central to Tillich's "Theology of Culture," where authentic religious experience is found amidst the triadic interplay of content, form, and meaning (*Gehalt*), to which he links the terms autonomy, heteronomy, and theonomy. *Content* denotes something objective in its simple existence. The act of giving *form* to content creates a recognizable structure within the cultural sphere. *Meaning* is something else again: it is the depth-meaning, the spiritual substance of a cultural product. In a traditional formulation of Tillich's paradigm, content is something we have no control over and arises in our midst, meaning is essential to human flourishing and is the only way that content and form offer evidence of the sacred, and form mediates between content and import and gives humans the ability to make meaning of that which surrounds us. Think of a river for example. When we picture a river in our minds, often we think of the rush of waters, the curve of the path, and various sounds erupting from the flow. Yet without river banks there would be only flooding and chaos. And without some memory as to what a river is and how a river relates to other things—a toaster, a checkerboard, a milkshake—we wouldn't know how to afford it value. In this way, the content of a flowing river is made possible for us through the form that is given it from the river banks, and the memories and contexts of rivers in our past and those we have heard about give meaning and depth to the content of "river" beyond a mere term. For Tillich, the balance of these three is necessary for that which is considered of religious value to be meaningful for human devotion. Faith communities will often place the emphasis or accent upon one or more aspects of this triad to the diminishment of the others. As will be discussed later in the chapter, the accent placed on this formulation methodologically *vis-à-vis* the Emergent church movement is often a therapeutic one whereby the content of cultural engagement is deeply *subjective* rather than *objective*.

---

23. Kimbell, *Emerging Church*, 105.

In this "neo-correlational" turn, the Tillichian methodology is employed in the manner described by Stephen Pattison as a "critical conversation" rather than a "critical correlation"—in short, culture has something to say—let them who have ears, hear.[24] As one reads through the ever-burgeoning literature surrounding the Emerging church movement, it is evident the form of the church found in many Christian communities is becoming more and more inadequate. Meaning in its overflowing abundance shatters the form meant to contain it. In the introduction to *Alternative Worship: Resources from and for the Emerging Church*, getting at this meaning is akin to a hammer pounding out a new form—a "hammering out what it is to be the gathered people of God—postscientism, postrationalism, and, most importantly, post-Christendom; what it is to worship God when gods are ubiquitous and every god-story, valid."[25] This "hammering out" of form via the overabundant surplus of valid "god-story" is akin to Tillich's notion of the authentically pre-eminent form of religiously charged cultural products readily shattering and reforming.

In this regard, let me outline three Tillichian returns foundational to most Emergent discourse, which are implied but not overtly noted in Emergent discourse yet remain engrafted to a distinct Tillichian heritage and the contemporary Emergent resonance

1. Schleiermacher's notion of "feeling" as an authentic categorical form of knowledge forged through radical reflexivity is the proper domain for authentic mission in the Emergent movement.

2. As underscored in Tillich's *Theology of Culture*, the church as "emergent" is profoundly *imminent and therefore necessarily social, positivistic, and historical.*

3. Theological anthropology is understood primarily through our *freedom* over and (at times) against the necessity of *redemption.*

First, for Schleiermacher receptivity to the fullness that God has in store for humanity is possible in immediate self-consciousness, or "feeling," which is the proper domain of authentic faith.

This *metanoia* or repenting from holding the priority of reason and rationalism as the mark of authentic faith in the Emergent move-

24. For a good introduction to Pattison's model of critical conversation, seek Pattison, "Some Straw."

25. Baker and Gay, *Alternative Worship*, 16.

ment has numerous reference points, but the corrective turn taken by Schleiermacher in reference to Kantian metaphysics is akin to the anti-Enlightenment turn taken by the Emergent movement and is therefore important to review. To put it simply, with Schleiermacher to "feel" is as valued in faith as "knowing." As mentioned earlier, this heritage of the inward, affective turn of radical subjectivity is rooted in the notable quotation by St. Augustine: *Noli foras ire, in teipsum redi; in interiore homine habitat veritas* ("Do not go abroad. Return within yourself. In the inward man dwells truth.").[26] Augustine is in line with Plato before him in his search for a unifying principle under and throughout the oppositions and complex divisions of the world. But Augustine draws a new direction in his avocation of *in interiore homine* as the *habitat veritas*. Dwelling in this modality of being in a radically reflexive repose, Augustine is not a precursor to the Cartesian philosophical turn where one "thinks themselves thinking" but the Schleiermachian turn of "feeling ourselves feeling."

Schleiermacher claims similarly that "feeling" is the mode of receptivity in which humans are both open to the interactions between rationality (mind) and sentience (being) as well as open to the absolute ground of those interactions. He defines feeling as "immediate self-consciousness," which removes feeling from the sphere of changeable emotions to the deeper one of what Heidegger will later call "fundamental moods" (*Stimmungen*) and Tillich will call "ultimate concern." Schleiermacher holds that feeling is not merely subjective self-awareness, but is genuinely intentional—it points us to not merely ourselves, but toward that in which, noting St. Paul's praxiological devotional refrain in Acts, "we live and move and have our being." An intuition of what is felt always accompanies feeling. As such, feeling is the primordial unity of subject-object interactions. Feeling is the proper domain of the primordially receptive nature of human being. In the way, feeling as it "emerges" is the proper domain of authentic mission in the recovery of the unity of subject-object relations both within ourselves and beyond as a call to and for the world.

Secondly, as with Tillich's summation of a Theology of Culture, *to be an "emergent" church is necessarily to be social, positive, and historical.*

In the fourth of his *Speeches*, Schleiermacher says, "Once there is religion, it must necessarily be social. That not only lies in human na-

26. Augustine, "De vera Religione," 262.

ture but also is preeminently in the nature of religion."[27] In this regard, human beings have a desire to communicate religious emotions and meanings to each other. From this communitarian interplay, historical religious communities arise. Accordingly, emergent forms of mission are therefore infinite and immeasurable by this understanding, but in addition, authentic mission must, akin to Schleiermacher's argument regarding religion, have a principle of individualization in itself, for otherwise it could not exist at all and be perceived.[28] According to this principle, mission cannot appear in the world as such—there is no natural form of mission. Mission necessarily appears in the world as a concrete historical community as vocation—a "called out" (or "thrown out" in Heideggarian language) community that forms and overcomes divisions between the self and the other and the self and God. Moreover, there is necessarily a plurality of authentic mission forms and practices; that is, a multi-valiant understanding of a theology of mission which draws from and supports a myriad of sources, based upon the plurality of possible intuitions and feelings enmeshed in the diverse firmament we find ourselves (and are found) in. As Schleiermacher notes in *On Mission: Speeches to Its Cultural Despisers*, he applauds rather than laments the condition of pluralism that exists among the multiplicity of human communities.

Thirdly, the Emergent church's mission aligns itself with Tillich via his reading of Schleiermacher through an essentialist theological anthropology that grounds and empowers a finite human freedom under the sovereignty of an infinitely free and loving God.

For many who would identify themselves as Emergent communities, radical human freedom is not only acknowledged but celebrated—we are created to be free . . . but from what and for what? Schleiermacher rigorously argues that human freedom is ultimately a limited, finite, and relative freedom, in contrast to Kant's moral philosophy. Similarly, the Emergent movement in its various communities of gathering holds in common a high value placed on a robust liberty core to humanity, which challenges both Reformed and Wesleyan notions of atonement. As seen throughout the eighteenth and nineteenth centuries, the notion of transcendental freedom stands at the center of both Kant's theoretical and practical critiques. For Kant, transcendental freedom is the non-contradictory idea of

27. Schleiermacher, *On Religion*, 98.
28. Ibid., 134.

an absolute beginning point out from which a rational subject (or moral agent) can produce an object (an action as a real state of affairs) quite independently of the natural nexus of cause and effect. As rational beings we are conscious of ourselves as acting and thereby bringing about new states of affairs within the totality of the world and its causal structure.

Therefore, according to Kant, the fact that humans intervene in the causal structure requires transcendental freedom as its necessary condition—we have liberty to change the world. In addition, we humans are conscious that we are accountable for our actions, which implies that we are conscious of an *a priori* moral norm by which we measure the moral worth of what is. As rational beings we can reflect on the felt oughtness that obligates us, and we can deduce the supreme principle of morality, the moral law, along with the categorical form of its imperative. What is more, we can test the moral worth of our actions by universalizing our maxims in accordance with universal and necessary condition of the possibility of any moral accountability and of any moral action. The central point for us is that Kant identifies the essence of religion with morality. To be religious is to understand the moral law as if it were a divine command. Religious experience for Kant is to feel reverence for the moral law. In contrast, Schleiermacher offers a stark alternative, which is carried forward into the legacy of Emergent neo-correlational theology.

In his early essay on human freedom (*Über die Freiheit*), Schleiermacher abandoned the idea of transcendental freedom in favor of a more limited notion of freedom ultimately grounded in the religious response to the infinite whole as it reveals itself in finite reality. Put another way, we are not merely free to be free, but free for a particular, incarnate purpose in this life. In contrast to Kant, Schleiermacher turned to the empirical experience of the moral agent. Schleiermacher argued against Kant that action is always determined by our strongest desire, that human action is moved by instincts or impulses. But that does not mean that reason is impotent in its deliberations about choices. He claimed that there is a properly moral impulse within the actual life experience of the empirical self. This moral impulse competes with other impulses in the deliberations of the agent to become the incentive of action. The originating cause of moral action therefore lies within the empirical self, rather than outside it. With this early critique of Kant's idea of transcendental freedom, Schleiermacher brought together what Kant had previously argued—namely, the nexus of sensible inclinations and moral duty—by making the moral impulse one of the affective desires that can determine a moral act. In so doing Schleiermacher did not deny the moral law, but rather claimed that the law is given through the sentient experience of the self and must be interpreted by it. This move is consistent with the previous steps in maneuvering between idealism and empiricism-positivism.

This level of unbridled imminent freedom as the foundational aspect of our humanity informs Emergent church writers in regard to their unilateral correlational methodology, which begins with a focus on what worshipping individuals and congregations "want and need" and then articulates a theology that responds to and fulfills those wants and needs through a call to human freedom toward others and God. In this way the correlation model drawn from Tillich attempts to find a better way of making Christian mission meaningful and relevant both to the congregation and to the culture at large. Drawing upon recent re-imaginings of the Celtic tradition, the Emergent movement argues for a theology of mission that is contrasted with what they term the "Roman model" of "finding out what God says" and then applying it to specific human situations. Such a traditional approach (what Dan Kimbell terms the "consumer church" model) is seen as dictatorial and restrictive, allowing no room for human meaning and response, and, more importantly, ignoring the complex web of reality that human beings already inhabit, and into which the theologian is attempting to speak the knowledge of God.

Don Browning—Acknowledging the Context of Our Selfless Identity

In a similar vein of post-evangelical critique of the modern church brought forward by the Emergent church movement, Don Browning in *A Fundamental Practical Theology* responded to this perceived deficiency of authenticity in practice by detailing a thorough practice-to-theory-to-practice Tillichian model for a theology of mission within three specific local congregations that predates the Emergent movement yet bears important points of contemporary reference.

Browning spends some time in *A Fundamental Practical Theology* justifying both the necessity of congregational studies and of the practical theology with which such studies are associated. He suggests that religious communities carry a sense of tradition or "group memory" that often serves to balance the corrosive effects of modern Western individualism. They are, in this sense, carriers of a crucial "practical wisdom." He writes,

> Western societies are desperate to find ways to make shared and workable decisions about the common good and the common life. The twin realities of modernity and liberalism have worked against the maintenance of shared traditions, social narratives, and communal identities. When it comes time to decide an issue about the common good, shared assumptive worlds are so fragmented that struggle, often unproductive, invariably ensues. . . . [After bouncing between the two poles of blind custom or purely theoretical theology], we now have returned to the category of the practical in search of a shared praxis that will enable us to either reconstruct tradition or learn to exercise our practical wisdom without it. These seem to be the two basic choices. In each case—the exercise of practical wisdom With or Without tradition—the debate is over competing images of what is variously called practical wisdom, practical reason, or *phronēsis*.[29]

Browning elaborates on this idea of tradition by contrasting a "popular" view of theology with what has actually developed in contemporary theological circles. For Browning, many academics have formed theology into a mysterious and arcane discipline, and to speak of such a thing as "practical theology" conjures up echoes of "practical astrology" or "practical alchemy." Akin to Emergent self-understanding, practical theology as articulated by Browning is to be a reflection on the historical self-understanding of a particular religious tradition, a reflection that wrestles with expressions of faith that involve myth, story, symbol, and metaphor. Browning notes by way of contrast the neo-orthodox theology of Karl Barth, which, while more contemporary than the Scholastics, still involves the authoritative model of God's self-disclosure to a receptive (meaning "passive") Christian church. By way of analogy, think of a physician who prescribes a cure for a patient without actually going through the careful rigors of a full medical diagnosis. This authoritative model, which Browning implicitly rejects, actually finds its way back into his congregational studies at several key points. He refers to Barth in this regard in support of his core thesis:

> Although contemporary theology is less rationalistic, it may not seem less apodictic, impractical, and unrelated to the aver-

29. Browning, *Fundamental Practical Theology*, 3–4.

age person. A theologian as recent as Karl Barth saw theology as the systematic interpretation of God's self-disclosure to the Christian church (Barth 1936, 47–70). There was no role for human understanding, action, or practice in the construal of God's self-disclosure. In this view, theology is practical only by applying God's revelation as directly and purely as possible to the concrete situations of life. The theologian moves from revelation to the human, from theory to practice, and from revealed knowledge to application. [30]

Notice that the term "revelation" is fused to the terms "apodictic" (incontrovertibly true), "theory," "impractical," and "unrelated to the average person." It is placed in direct opposition to human understanding, action, and practice. Curiously enough, however, when Browning later recounts a series of analytical descriptions of a failing church congregation, he observes that each description, while striving for objectivity, implicitly compares the congregation to an ideal of what a church should embody. I would argue here in passing that such a normative ideal is only possible if we incorporate at least a few bricks from traditional revelatory theology into our practical theological edifice.

Browning elaborates on his disagreement with Karl Barth by observing, along with hermeneutical writers such as Hans-Georg Gadamer, that the theologian does not approach God, Scripture, and the historic witness of the church like an empty slate or a Lockean *tabula rasa*, waiting to be plugged in to a concrete situation like some kind of announcing angel. Akin to the voicing of Emergent thinkers, Browning would argue that we are already situated within a specific time and culture, bringing to the texts and practices of our faith a whole complex of often unquestioned assumptions. He uses the term "theory-laden" to describe these assumptions and practices, pointing out that

> [w]e are so embedded in our practices, take them so much for granted, and view them as so natural and self-evident that we never take time to abstract the theory from the practice and look at it as something in itself.[31]

This changes when a religious community hits a crisis of some kind. As a community moves from stasis to paradox and liminality, it begins

30. Ibid., 5.
31. Ibid., 6.

to ask questions about its practices that seem to be failing. It attempts to describe these practices from a variety of viewpoints in order to understand the questions precipitated by the crisis. Eventually, the community re-examines the texts and events that constitute the sources of the norms and ideals that guide its practices, questioning its own inherited tradition and normative sources in light of the questions engendered by the crisis. Here the decision is often made whether to find new possibilities and interpretations from within the tradition or break with the past and look for answers outside of traditional boundaries. Browning notes that traditional or "confessionally oriented" communities may stop here, while more critically oriented groups may go on to devise various tests for the practical adequacy of these new meanings. Finally, these new meanings and practices are implemented and continue until the next crisis, whereupon the whole process begins again. To use Browning's phraseology, the movement is from *a crisis of present theory-laden practice* to *a retrieval of normative theory-laden practice* to *the creation of a more critically held theory-laden practice*. In short, theology is re-envisioned as a movement from practice to theory and back again to practice.

What remains to be seen therefore in the current Emergent church movement is whether or not an approach re-imagined as "neo-correlational theology," drawing upon the tradition of Tillich and Browning, tacitly relies upon a more traditional theology that it explicitly rejects. The challenge addressed by Browning and intimated throughout Tillich's profound reflections on culture is the difficulty in maintaining that praxio-centric nexus of engaging traditions of faith and the immediacy of culturally grounded mission without becoming traditionalism *par excellence*.

With the rising awareness and affirmation that the postmodern age is the age of the neo-pagan—is the Emergent church movement only flirting with liberty and a release from formalism toward authentic engagement with meaning through content, only to fall back into modern concepts and practices that reinforce that which they seem intent on moving beyond?[32] Granted, there is a mass turning away in Protestantism from humanistic rationalism to pre-modern religions (seen in such movements as Radical Orthodoxy and Ancient-Future Faith[33]), spirituali-

32. See Adams, "Possibilities for Theology"; Harvey, *Condition of Postmodernity*; and Berry and Wernak, *Shadow of Spirit*.

33. See Milbank, Pickstock, Ward, eds., *Radical Orthodoxy*; and Webber, *Ancient-Future Faith*, respectively.

ties within the established religions, and the syncretistic spiritualities that meld any blend of spiritualities of an individual's choice. Tillich describes this context in *The Protestant Era* as a *Kairos* moment: "But an age that is turned toward, and open to, the unconditional is one in which the consciousness of the presence of the unconditional permeates and guides all cultural functions and forms. The divine, for such a state of mind, is not a problem but a presupposition. Its 'givenness' is more certain than that of anything else."[34] Whether the Emergent churches understandings of the Christian life can maintain this vision remains to be seen. That said, as we proceed in this exploration of the identity formation of the Emergent self, we will see that true identity will never be contained within institutions alone—it is in mission to and for those God calls us to, regardless of institutional allegiance, that will mark the channel by which we journey in and through the kingdom of God.

34. Tillich, *Protestant Era*, 43.

5

Forging the Kenotic Self through
the Responsibility to the Face of the Other

So he had sunk to the state of a beast that licks his chaps after meat.
This was the end: and a faint glimmer of fear began to pierce the fog
of his mind. He pressed his face against the pane of the window and
gazed out into the darkening street. Forms passed this way and that
way through the dull light. And that was life. . . . His soul was fat-
tening and congealing into a gross grease, plunging ever deeper in its
dull fear into a sombre threatening dusk, while the body that was his
stood, listless and dishonoured, gazing out of darkened eyes, helpless,
perturbed and human for God to stare upon.[1]

WHAT IS THE LOCATION and purpose of the kenotic self? In Irish
writer James Joyce's 1916 novel *A Portrait of the Artist as a Young
Man*, we see the character of Stephen Dedalus, a young artist in early
twentieth-century Dublin, slipping further and further into self-loathing.
As in the quote that opens this chapter, we hear the base carnality of
Stephen as he stands in the world—exposed to humans and God alike—
fully "himself," yet lacking any sense of meaning beyond survival. Is it
enough to be forming and becoming in responsiveness to the neo-pagan,
cyberpunk culture around us, the deep call within us, and the mission
of God as seen through and with the church? In taking seriously the
Great Commandment of Jesus, this chapter will explore the ground of
the kenotic self as a forging of identity through deep and abiding responsibility for others. As Jesus commanded, "You shall love the Lord your
God with all your heart, mind, soul and strength; and you shall love your
neighbor as yourself." If this is the great command of our Lord, it is also

---

1. Joyce, *Portrait of the Artist*, 105.

the great ground of the kenotic self. In this regard, we will explore the role that categories of personhood[2] and community drawn from streams of Continental philosophical thought can play in creating a bridge for dialogue between various theological concerns in regard to what constitutes a sustainable identity after God and a sense of self for and with others in culture. To do this, we will briefly explore a philosophical heritage that includes such voices in Continental philosophy as Paul Ricouer, Emmanuel Lévinas, Jacques Derrida, and Jean Luc Marion, and which is indebted also to Husserl, Heidegger, and Hegel.

Most theologies in relation to the self continue to draw their theoretical form from German Idealist traditions that are static and immovable, thereby encouraging a theology that is unable to dialogue with other voices and ultimately unable (and unwilling) to hear the still, small voices of divine revelation. In the phenomenological tradition there resides a common presupposition that signification—our lived lives we experience with our senses—always precedes and intends the signifying activity of our conscious mind—the idealized and transcendent notion of what it means to be alive. In this way, phenomenological discussions of what it means to be human challenge analytical abstraction, isolation, or examination of the action of signification, which would result in reifying or mystifying our understanding outside of the lived experience. In short, the phenomenological tradition provides a helpful philosophical framework for bringing the questions of what it means to be a self down to the level that everyone can participate in. As will be explored in this chapter, the works of Paul Ricouer, Emmanuel Lévinas, and Jacques Derrida provide a welcome choir of voices in addition to traditional Western theological methodologies. Bring this choir together in correlation with contemporary culture offers us a revisioning of how cultural identity is understood and appropriated that is deeply abiding in Scriptural reflection, theologically orthodox tradition, open to hearing lived common human experience, and receptive to deep imagination and creativity.

---

2. Some philosophical traditions will speak of "personhood" as a distinct category from "human being." Personhood denotes moral agency and responsibility, while the designation "human being" in philosophical traditions is the distinct organism. In this regard, questions of personhood and human being are seen as distinct ethical and moral categories. I am addressing the notion of personhood from the theological tradition of *imago Dei*, which is an incarnational and holistic designation and does not distinguish between body, mind, and spirit.

In philosopher Paul Ricoeur's project, the human subject is conceptualized on two axes: a horizontal axis, which constitutes the cultural and social matrix defining the self by its context; and a vertical axis, which is the subject's position in time. The narrative life is plotted out inside this social/temporal grid. Ricoeur's methodology integrates the two prevailing Western philosophical schools: Anglo-American analytical philosophy and Continental phenomenological philosophy. His analytical approach to phenomenology (or phenomenological approach to linguistic analysis) results in a synthesis of these two divergent schools, and creates something of a hermeneutical phenomenology. Such an approach appears to be a more integrative and all-encompassing approach to subjectivity than either taken alone, or results in a more robust and less reduced picture of the subject.

For Ricoeur, being-in-the-world (similar to what we are calling the "kenotic self") is something that is mysterious, intangible, and perceived through experience. It is therefore not a "problem" as such, but it is a mystery, and it is this allowing for mystery and possibility that gives way to identity grounded in faith rather than certainty.[3] This aspect of mystery that draws the subject into deep and abiding faith is a necessary aspect of the authentic kenotic self. For Ricoeur, the analysis of being is the analysis of experience, and seeks to answer the how of being more so than that what of being. This approach to being is tackled by Ricoeur through his commitment to a deep, intentional concern for authenticity. His anthropology—what constitutes true humanity—does not proceed from the simple to the complex, but always moves within the totality of being itself.

The philosopher Emmanuel Lévinas, who was a contemporary of Ricoeur, was undeniably a central figure in the development of Ricoeur's position on *alterity*—the thinking about what it means to be a self through the eyes of the other. Lévinas's concept of the other as "facing" the self, is similar to the idea of the "summoned subject" in Ricoeur.[4] In Lévinas,

---

3. Granted, philosophers such as Lévinas and Derrida are going to be suspicious of the intoning use of "mystery" as it is traditionally understood. The use of "mystery" can seem to defer responsibility to and for the other. However, the theological notion of the *mysterion* is not a deferral of responsibility, but the call of responsibility in its fullest sense.

4. For Lévinas, this "facing" is only in the sense of asymmetrically commanding me from on high. This is not reciprocal intersubjectivity *per se*, but rather the full summons of the subject by the other.

the other comes from outside, in the form of an epiphany that overflows categories of meaning, and "faces" or summons the self to response. The difference between compelling and summoning seems to underscore a sense that a response is naturally elicited. As will be further discussed in this chapter, Eastern and Western conceptions of the subject include the notion that what we are calling the kenotic self is always "faced into being" from the other.[5] It is in the philosophical tradition of Ricouer and Lévinas if applied to the ways in which the kenotic self is summoned into being by the other (be it the divine or human other) to realize its desire to be by responding to the voice of the other. This is an event of authentic identity found only in the summons of the other—akin to revelation—or "moments of emergence" rather than strategic conditional moves by the self. In summation, this chapter will propose Lévinas' threefold movement of astonishment, proximity, and substitution as a helpful methodology for a revisioned missional theology after open theism.

Jacques Derrida and the Kenotic Self as "Radically (De)Centric"

It is interesting to reconsider Jacques Derrida, whose passing in 2004 marked a renewed interest in his philosophical *oeuvre*, since, while he was resolutely determined not to be considered a "religious" writer, he actually brings profound and insightful philosophical insight to the task of contemporary missional thought and praxis. Going back to Derrida's earlier work, in particular the seminal essay "Structure, Sign, and Play in the Discourse of the Human Sciences," found in the collected essays on literature entitled *Writing and Difference*, Derrida offers a bold challenge to essentialist discourse yet also a reflective opportunity to relocate what is understood as identity away from a centered sense of selfhood and toward a radically decentered and ultimately "otherly" natured ground for being. Key to this radically decentric move is the deconstruction of essential categories in favor of authenticity.

As Derrida notes, "the history of metaphysics, like the history of the West, is the history of these metaphors and metonymies."[6] Derrida goes on to state that "we have no language—no syntax and no lexicon—which

---

5. It is important to note that to Lévinas, the notion of self is ultimate a chimera given that there is no self but the summoning of the other, and the self's desire is not for the self to be *per se*, but the self toward the other. See esp. Lévinas, *Otherwise than Being*.

6. Derrida, *Writing and Difference*, 279.

is foreign to this history" of metaphors and metonymies."[7] For example, in claims such as seeing the sign/signifier "Jesus" as the "historical Jesus," the "kerygmatic Jesus," the "apocalyptic Jesus," the "liberation Jesus," or for our purposes in this book "the kenotic Jesus," we must realize that it is only being in the form of *metaphors* and *metonymies*—language that points toward the event horizon of the Living Christ, and not the substitute for him. Although metaphors claim to state that "this is that," or while metonymies, as the root indicates, make possible changes of names ("we will now re-name this to be called that"), they are merely descriptions and can become barriers. This is central to Derrida's project in "Structure, Sign, and Play," in his argument that we need to look beyond our need in Western metaphysics to "fight for the determination of Being *as presence* in all senses of this word. It could be shown that all the names related to fundamentals, to principles, or to the center have always designated an invariable presence—*eidos, archē, telos, energeia, ousia* (essence, existence, substance, subject) *alētheia*, transcendentality, consciousness, God, man, and so forth."[8]

In "Structure, Sign and Play," Derrida is seeking to situate ultimate subjectivity—that which we call our identity or sense of purpose—as it is to be determined by a given subject, in a place beyond language. In essence, ultimate meaning and purpose is something we point at through language not something we can ever capture or tie down to a particular doctrine—the Word does indeed become flesh as that in which we "live and move and have our being." Seeking not to destroy the subject, Derrida states that his wish is to "situate it . . . [this ultimately is] a question of knowing where it [the subject] comes from."[9] In this way, the origin of a subject before language is "named" by it, prior to seeking definition of pre-existent terms. This point of origin is where one draws meaning from the "history of meanings" that forms our understanding. This is what Derrida terms "center."

Jean Hyppolite, author of *Logic and Existence*,[10] posed the question to Derrida regarding his lecture on "Structure, Sign, and Play" as to "what

7. Ibid., 280.

8. Ibid.

9. Ibid., 278.

10. Hyppolite, *Logic & Existence.*

a center might mean."[11] In Hyppolite's words, is "the center the knowledge of general rules which, after a fashion, allow us to understand the interplay of the elements? Or is the center certain elements which enjoy a particular privilege with the ensemble?"[12] Derrida's answer was as follows: "I don't mean to say that I thought of approaching an idea by which this loss of the center that would be an affirmation."[13] The center of which he speaks is not a certain place as we shall see, not a place to be affirmed and locked into meaning, for this would do to the word "center" what Derrida says the term now does—make a "substitution of linguistic center for true center"—so that "the center receives different forms or names" and we ultimately lose that which we seek. Derrida's definition of "center" constitutes abstracted definitions of a communally concerned identity: "The center, which is by definition unique, constituted that very thing within a structure which while governing that structure, escapes structurality."[14]

In the fight to define, definition in its truest sense is lost. For example, when reflection about what grounds our identity moves from engaged thought and praxis to being inscribed into what we term "doctrine" or "theology," this move can become a form of dominant discourse that has the exclusive role and location for the spiritual formation in people's lives, which can actually overturn the basic claims of Christianity itself—the Word become flesh becoming words of theological rhetoric. As noted by David Tracy,[15]

> The [church] lives in a strange and healing paradox disclosed . . . throughout the scriptures: so deeply into one's existence does the unmasking radicality of the Word strike that the radical contingency and ambiguity of all culture, all civilization, all institutions, even nature itself [in sum, the "world"] are unmasked by the same Word which commands and enables work for the world, and more concretely for the neighbor. This Christian insight into the conventionality, the arbitrariness, the radical contingency of all culture, all nature and all institutions has a reverse side: the radical ambiguity

11. Macksey and Donato, *Structuralist*, 265. Lee Morrissey makes interesting comparisons between the questions raised by Derrida in "Structure, Sign, and Play" and the political undertones of the essay; see Morrissey, "Derrida."

12. Hyppolite, *Logic & Existence*.

13. Ibid.

14. Derrida, *Writing and Difference*, 279.

15. I am using the notion of the collective church as comparable to Tracy's use of the individual.

of all culture, nature, institutions—all the world—and their constant temptation to self-aggrandizement and self-delusion. Yet this very same insight into the radical contingency and real ambiguity of the world posits itself not only by negating all "worldly" pretensions to divinity, atemporality, eternity, but also by positing the command and the possibility of living in and for this contingent, ambiguous, created and divinely beloved "world."[16]

Tracy goes on to say that "rather than repeating the domesticated slogans that presume to capture this dialectic ("The [church] is in the world, but not of it"), it seems more correct to say that the [church] is released from the world, for the world."[17]

This can be seen in the ongoing attempts within missiological studies, where the call to proclaim the gospel will have to continually fight the tendency to build walls and choose a fixed center of rhetoric and discourse rather than an organic, decentered one—a form and style of talking about the experience of what it means to share the gospel of Jesus with the current generation that is delimited, static, and closed, rather than one that provokes eschatological proclamation and parabolic enactment that will reverse every given form of what people have presupposed God's working in the world to be about. As Derrida notes, we seek delimited structures such as a closed and static form of language through a fixed, unchanging center point, which ultimately "neutralize[s] . . . [and] reduce[s]" the truth of a subject into merely "a point of presence, a fixed origin."[18] It is this false center then that controls, in the sense of containing, the structurality of the structure, reducing it. Thus the extremes—those points of engaging the presence of Christ that propel us beyond ourselves and our fears—are neutralized by the domesticated center.

In "Structure, Sign, and Play," Derrida emphasizes that true center is "not a fixed locus but a function."[19] In one sense, then, centering as function—or import, to recall Paul Tillich's category discussed in the previous chapter—need not be put in one place; the function can be distributed *throughout* the structure. This is another way of understanding that the center is not the center; the center as import or pure meaning and purpose need not be at the central place or a central doctrine—rather, the Center

16. Tracy, *Analogical Imagination*, 48.

17. Ibid.

18. Derrida, *Writing and Difference*, 278.

19. Ibid., 280.

which is Christ is always moving toward, through, and even beyond us. Another way of saying this is that rather than working at mapping a fixed point for the locus of meaning, we need to be prepared for the Center of all meaning to find and locate us in new and often mysterious ways. Moreover, if the center as ultimate meaning is not a central doctrine but the Word made flesh, then it is highly variable; not only can the function or import be fulfilled from different theological stances, but different entry means of accessing and being encountered by the Living God need to be allowed for. On the notion of the radical center, Derrida states that "[i]f this is so, the entire history of the concept of structure, before the rupture of which we are speaking, must be thought of as a series of substitutions of center for center."[20] In short, the functionality of what is "center" is itself just a substitute for a previous center; the function remains the same even if the center has moved.

This power to contain true identity through centering, essentialist language is, on the one hand, rhetorical, yet on the other hand, substantial and real. But words do not necessarily establish what the object is; they instead participate in "a history of meanings."[21] This is nothing new to those who have spent significant time on the mission field; in translating theological terms such as "forgiveness," "salvation," or "sin," such concepts need to be unpacked of their culturally embedded traditions and allowed to find a locus of meaning in the culture such concepts find themselves in. Moreover, to make a claim of identity based on signifiers such as "the missional Jesus" takes the form of both metaphor ($x = y$, or "this" is "that") and metonymy (a name change; Christ is now the Nazarene), so that the import or event horizon of meaning sought through form and content may still be different from what either the metaphor or the metonymy can suggest. The face we may seek to present—the authentic Jesus—is not to be found. The face we do figure, as Derrida notes in reference to Lévinas' work, "is neither the face of God nor the figure of man: it is their resemblance. A resemblance which, however, we must think before, or without, the assistance of the Same."[22] We who seek this "face" are in the space that is the difference between the same and the other. It is in this space that Lévinas sees the restoration of abiding peace—here the summons of the

20. Ibid., 278.
21. Ibid., 279.
22. Derrida, Writing and Difference, 109.

other is possible, and we are called outside of ourselves. "We live in and of difference," according to Derrida. If Derrida's assertion is true, where does ultimate meaning reside, particularly in relation to the question of the kenotic self?

For Derrida, given this distinction drawn between true identity and metaphor, it is to be concluded that identity—the kenotic self—ultimately only exists in "difference" between meaning and the label placed upon it. Akin to our discussion of Goethe's morphological self in the previous chapters, these labels of metaphors and metonymies only have meaning in their ability to assuage and master a certain degree of anxiety—probably the anxiety of difference, which is also the anxiety of similarity. Anxiety as to what lies behind the veil of signifiers such as "the historical Jesus," in whatever manifestation, forces institutions to double efforts to reinterpret terms as well as look through these signs to what is beyond. This shift, according to Derrida, is the point of "rupture." "Rupture . . . come[s] about when the structurality of structure had to begin to be thought."[23] This rupture frees us from the mere repetition of categories that limit meaning, or what Derrida refers to as iteration. Once we begin to recognize that the structure of any given sign is merely a structure, and nothing else, a rupture can occur. Derrida claims that "perhaps something has occurred in the history of the concept of structure that could be called an event," where "its exterior form would be that of a rupture."[24] Prior to this realization, when people believe that the structure is something other than a structure, they have chosen a mere metaphor instead of import or meaning, and in short, have chosen form rather than true transformational encounter with the Living Christ.

According to cultural theorist Lee Morrissey, one way of framing Derrida's attempt in "Structure, Sign, and Play" could be understood as part of what Hal Foster in *Return of the Real* describes as "a shift in conception—from reality as an effect of representation to the real as a thing of trauma."[25] That is, the "real" is something that is beyond critique as "the traumatic" is beyond category and escapes language altogether. Another way to view this is Lévinas's notion in *Otherwise than Being* that there is an

---

23. Derrida, *Writing and Difference*, 280.

24. Macksey and Donato, *Structuralist Controversy*, 278.

25. Foster, *Return of the Real*, 146.

ethical echo prior to the sound.[26] This "shift in conception" is an attempt to see with reality, not merely to form a reality to be seen. Similarly, to resolve the question of presenting the call of the gospel today, a rupture is needed in the false ways that meaning is made and supported. The reality that there is no institution—be it the church, mission agency, or the academy—whose task it is to preserve separate fixed centering points needs to be affirmed. Rather, all are part of a larger enterprise whose "center" is shared beyond definition. This is a racially centric calling toward seeking and proclaiming "Jesus who was the first truly apocalyptic prophet, the one who first enacted a total apocalyptic ending—but an apocalyptic ending that is apocalyptic beginning, a beginning that has been renewed again and again by those who embody him, or those who embody his acts and words."[27]

In short, Derrida's critique of the centering aspects of Western thought provide a powerful call to humility for those of us committed to proclaiming the gospel, and an invitation to see ourselves as kenotic. How easy and tempting it is to weight the message of the gospel's reception within a given missional context upon the phrases or slogans of our traditions rather than patiently waiting upon the Living Christ to awaken from a cultural malaise—an awakening that may mean we ourselves may be silenced into wonder and praise. How comfortable has the church become in its time-proven rhetoric for salvation, that we either ignore or become increasingly indifferent to the working of the Holy Spirit in our time!

In one interview Derrida stated that "what interests me today is not strictly called either literature or philosophy, I'm amused by the idea that my adolescent desire—let's call it that—should have directed me toward something in writing which was neither the one nor the other. What was it? 'Autobiography' is perhaps the least adequate name, because it remains for me the most enigmatic, the most open, even today."[28] Derrida is truly on to something here. This beginning point of dialogue and discovery of identity as kenotic self is an autobiographical engagement—what is our story and how should we be humbled by it in the face of those God calls into our midst?—that can situate and kenotically empty our preconceived assumptions as to the essential apparatus of conversations and encoun-

---

26. Lévinas, *Otherwise than Being.*

27. Altizer, *Contemporary Jesus,* 17.

28. Derrida, "This Strange Institution," 34.

ters in order to allow the silence and patient repose that waits both on God and needs of the culture we are called to. This is where I suggest the character of the kenotic self that is "radically centric" begins—at its most authentic point found in humility, kenosis of the self before others, and the patiently waiting repose before God's people which, in Derridian discourse, is the moment most "de-centered." This point, which is "the most enigmatic, the most open," is where sharing the gospel becomes an act of dynamic re-creating and encountering which brings an open and enigmatic authenticity that is at the heart of calling people to the person of Christ in truth and in love.

In this regard we now turn to a contemporary of Jacques Derrida, Emmanuel Lévinas, and reflect on how a "radically centric" notion of the kenotic self is further empowered through a "radical facing of the other."

Emmanuel Lévinas and the Face of the Other

As people who have been awakened to the deep and powerful calling of the gospel, what does it mean to be encountered as we face others with this powerful message of hope and reconciliation? The beginning point of this discussion turns on the basic yet profound question of how we relate to those who are "other." For philosopher Emmanuel Lévinas, this question is deeply grounded in ethics and how we relate to each other as people respected in the eyes of God. In short, to be a self is ultimately to be "ethical." For Lévinas, ethics is, first and foremost, born on the concrete level of person-to-person contact. He does not find the moral "ought" inscribed within the laws of the cosmos, in reason, or in any universal desire for pleasure. Instead, each particular instance of moral questioning produces the dynamic tension between what is right and wrong in and of itself.[29]

When asked how to define ethics, we are assuming that our answer will include an important reference to other people. This is not necessarily to say that there can be no ethics without at least two people—though this is the case for Lévinas, and is also core (if not an essential stance) within Judeo-Christian ethic formations from Augustine through figures such as

29. It is important to note at this juncture that philosophers working within Lévinas' writings do not view him as *prescriptive*—that he is somehow founding the subject on a pre-ontological relationality that constitutes "me" as a subject. Rather, Lévinas' project leans toward the *descriptive*—that my connection to the Other (*Autre*) already enjoins me to treat/not treat this Other in specific ways.

John Howard Yoder and the neo-Anabaptists, and John Milbank and the Radical Orthodox theologians, to name a few examples. In short, ethics is an important issue when we discuss what we mean by mission because it governs the way in which we relate with one another; we must have some understanding of how we live (ethics) if we are to fully appreciate and redeem what we understand to be the reason we live and die (mission). As Kant's categorical imperative indicates, the imperative exercised over us by virtue of being thoughtful individuals or moral agents is always to treat all humanity, whether one's own person or another, not only as a means but also as an end in and of itself. And philosopher John Stuart Mill's "principle of utility" implies an essential link to persons other than ourselves—referred to throughout this section as "the other"—in framing ethics as being rooted in the notion of the greatest happiness for the greatest number, not merely the individual. If ethics is concerned with the other, then it would appear that, in order to fill out a complete account of ethics, the means by which two or more people come into contact with each other will be vitally important. In summary, it can be argued that the basis of Lévinas's ethical project is as follows: to establish the source of contact between persons or the source of interpersonal meaning, and in finding this meaning, find the ethical.

While Lévinas has been considered a fellow traveler alongside the philosophical nonfoundationalist tradition called deconstruction, it is also important to remember that Lévinas situates himself not on the margins of traditional ethics, but in the logical progression that comes directly out of the tradition established by Descartes, Kant, and Husserl, who sought to solve the dilemma of how our ideals should be lived out in the world of flesh. "Every idea is a work of the mind," writes Descartes in his *Meditations*.[30] Ideas are created, invented by a mind, not discovered. This leaves Descartes with a problem: "How can [ideas] that have their origin in the mind nevertheless give us knowledge of independently real substances."[31] He answers this question through proofs for God's existence—the existence of God provides the overarching bridge by which self and other, in retaining distinct identities, can have the possibility of connection. But as the philosophical tradition progresses after Descartes, Kant notes that God cannot be used within philosophy to the extent that

30. Descartes, *Meditations*, 162.
31. Wolff, *Kant's Theory*, 32.

Descartes would like. For Kant, the inversion of subject and object occurs whereby God becomes the object of our consideration and thought rather than human beings being the object of God's consideration. Thus, Descartes is left alone in his world with only his ideas: there is no contact with "the other" who is not an other in one of his ideas. The phenomenological philosopher Edmund Husserl takes this to its logical consequence in the fifth of his *Cartesian Meditations* and notes that the other is "there," present to me, but only in the sense that the other is present before for me existentially. Husserl writes, "Consciousness makes present a 'there too', which nevertheless is not itself there and can never become an 'itself-there.'"[32] The other of Husserl's *Cartesian Meditations* is not an other who exists independently of me as in Lévinas's reflections; rather, the other is only the meaning that I constitute for the other. In other words, the meaning of being an other comes down to my *interpretation* of the other, an interpretation that is the working of my own mind quite apart from what or whether the other may be. In short, even as we move into the existential and phenomenological, encountering the other remains predicated upon the self as interpreter and ultimately arbitrator of not only identity but the meaning of that identity.

If we can accept this notion that our encounters with those other than ourselves begin with certain presupposed ideas regarding who they are, and that these ideas of the other are inventions of the mind—that ideas are, when it comes down to it, only interpretations of something—and if ethics, in fact, is taken to refer to real other persons who exist apart from my interpretations, then we are up against a problem: there is no way in which such ideas, in this current model, refer to independently existing other persons, and as such, ideas cannot be used to found an ethics. There can be no pure practical reason until after contact with the other is established.

Given this view of the self as the ultimate determiner of identity and meaning for the other, anytime we take the person we encounter in our idea to be the real person, we have closed off contact with the actual real person; we have cut off the connection with the other that is necessary if ethics is to refer to real other people. This becomes an important consideration for missions in so far as how we frame and ultimately encounter the other in relation to the call of mission and the radical nature of the

32. Husserl, *Cartesian Meditations*, 50, 139.

gospel message. If we approach cultural settings with presuppositions, we fall into the potential trap of framing our message and our understanding of the potential encounter in a way that allows no space for surprise nor for the possibility of revelation. This is a central violence to the other that denies the other his/her own autonomy. Lévinas calls this violence "totalization," which occurs whenever we limit the other to a set of rational or preconceived categories, be they cultural, racial, sexual, or otherwise. Indeed, it occurs whenever we already presuppose to know what the other is about before the other has even spoken. Totalization is a denial of the other's difference, the denial of the otherness of the other. That is, it is the inscription of the other in the same. If ethics presupposes the real other person, then such totalization will, in itself, be unethical.

If reducing the other to my sphere of ideas cuts off contact with the other, then we are presupposing that contact with the other has already been established. And if contact with the other cannot be established through ideas, then we must look elsewhere. Thus, Lévinas looks not to reason, but to sensibility, to find the real essence of the other.

Sensibility, for Lévinas, goes back to a point before thought originates, before the ordering of a world into a system or totality. Sensibility is a profound waiting, not an active seeking after, as is thought, and it finds its contextual grounding in joy. Life as it is lived (rather than understood) is lived as the satisfaction of being "filled" with sensations, the satisfaction of living and moving as a created person within the scope of creation.

Lévinas at this point seeks to deepen philosopher Martin Heidegger's project in relation to Heidegger's notion of "tool." Reading the earlier Heidegger in *Being and Time*, we find Heidegger maintaining that inauthentic *existenz* (the term Heidegger employs for "existence") contextualizes itself in the world of things by relating to things (including other people) as mere tools—devices to be used for a particular purpose. Furthering this argument, Lévinas maintains that we live from these things or people as *nourishments*—we do not merely seek to stand apart from them, but digest them into our self in an act of totalization. In the morning I eat my breakfast cereal; in the activity of eating it becomes a part of my body. In a similar fashion according to Lévinas, we digest the language and meaning of not only food and drink, but of cultural forms as well that evidently "feed" our identity. In the act of reading and/or listening to a work of art—say a novel, film, or musical performance—I do not stall for a hermeneutic or reflective repose prior to understanding;

I am engaged as one descending into a pool, not with a distanced objectivity providing passive reflection on the event. I "digest" the art. It becomes me. This "living from" is a matter of consumption, a matter of taking what is other and making it become a part of me. Lévinas writes,

> Nourishment, as a means of invigoration, is the transmutation of the other into the same, which is in the essence of enjoyment: an energy that is other, recognized as other, recognized . . . as sustaining the very act that is directed upon it, becomes, in enjoyment, my own energy, my strength, me.[33]

In a way, Lévinas resonates with cultural theorist Jean Baudrillard's correction of Marxist critique. Where Karl Marx argued that power is seen in and with those who control the modes of production, Baudrillard argues that power is seen and manifested in our role as consumers. This taking on of what nourishes me conveys a separation between me and what has yet to nourish me. "Enjoyment is made," writes Lévinas, "of the memory of its thirst; it is a quenching."[34] Enjoyment then includes the memory of once not having been satisfied with what now satisfies me. Thus, enjoyment also involves stepping back from my environment; "living from . . . delineates independence itself, the independence of enjoyment and of its happiness."[35] Before enjoyment, there is me and the other thing that has yet to nourish me, even if the otherness of what will nourish me becomes apparent only in enjoyment, in the "memory" of its thirst. I can represent bread, but this will not feed me. I must eat it. But then in eating bread, the memory of hunger demonstrates a separation between the bread and me. Thus, as Lévinas notes in his earlier work in regard to enjoyment, the self emerges already as the subject of its need.

If Lévinas is correct, then, the human being starts first as one motivated toward joy. This enjoyment—being summoned by joy as independence—is the initial formation of the "I." It is at this point that the Enlightenment seems to stall with the echo of Polonius's words to Laertes in Shakespeare's *Hamlet* (act 1, scene 3): "This above all: to thine ownself be true." But, this self, the self of enjoyment, constitutes egoism. It is happy, but selfish. The self of enjoyment journeys into the world to make everything other part of itself, and it succeeds very well at this task.

33. Lévinas, *Totality*, 111.
34. Ibid., 113.
35. Ibid., 110.

Richard Cohen summarizes Lévinas on this point:

> [Sensation] is called "happiness" because at this level of sensibility the subject is entirely self-satisfied, self-complacement [sic], content, sufficient. Instead of [rational] synthesis, there are vibrations; instead of unifications, there are excitations; rather than an ecstatic self, there are margins of intensities, scattered stupidities, involutions without centers—egoism and solitude without substantial unity; a sensational happiness. . . . This event does not happen to subjectivity, this eventfulness, this flux, is subjectivity.[36]

Thus, Lévinas finds on the level of sensibility a subjectivity that is more primordial than rational subjectivity. It is not limited by the sphere of one's own ideas, but by the egoist self that goes out to enjoy the world. What is important here is that, unlike the sphere of ideas, sensibility reaches further out into the domain of the extra-mental.[37]

Establishing subjectivity on the level of sensibility provides Lévinas with a "place" where the other can be met, not in the closed and hyper-reasoned rooms of interior consciousness, but on the street, in the classroom, or in the workplace, where the egoism of enjoyment has the possibility of becoming "filled" with sensations and ultimately creates a separated self that can be met by the other (*Autre*).[38] Furthermore, establishing subjectivity on the level of sensibility leads Lévinas to a point where he can establish that the human subject is, first and foremost, passive. Sensations come to me from the outside, unlike the Augustinian tradition of *Noli foras ire, in teipsum redi; in interiore homine habitat veritas* ("Do not go outward; return within yourself. In the inward man dwells truth."),[39] where they are only to be swallowed up on the inside. Unlike the contents of ideas, sensations are discovered, given and not merely invented.

The ethical moment, the moment in which the moral "ought" shows itself, is found, for Lévinas, on the level of sensibility when the egoist self comes across something that it wants to enjoy, something that it wants to make a part of itself, but cannot. In many respects this is the key moment of mission as well—when the self comes into contact with a true other that I acknowledge as being truly independent of me and outside my sphere

---

36. Cohen, *Lévinas*, 201.

37. Lévinas, *Totality and Infinity*, 109.

38. "The movement of separation is not on the same plane as the movement of transcendence." Lévinas, ibid., 148.

39. Augustine, "De vera Religione," 72.

of control. The choice becomes one between humility or dominance and control. That which the self wants to enjoy but cannot is the other person. The reason that it cannot enjoy the other person is not rooted in some deficiency of sensibility, but in the other person who pushes back, as it were, who does not allow him/herself to be consumed in the egoism of my enjoyment. The other resists consumption. The presence of the other, on this level, is not, properly speaking, known. The other person is encountered as a felt weight against me.

Thus, for Lévinas, the other has some power over me. Indeed, the other is a transcendence that comes from beyond the categories of my thought, from beyond the world, from the other side of being. Because of the otherworldliness of the epiphany of the other in the face-to-face encounter, the (other) face speaks thus: "I am not yours to be enjoyed: I am absolutely other," or to put it in Lévinas' terms, "thou shalt not kill."

Astonishment as Initial Approach in Finding the Kenotic Self

Commenting on Lévinas' view of the other, John Burke describes the initial approach of the other person in terms of astonishment or surprise. In so doing, he also notes the essential element of radical passivity that arises from contact with the other person. As Burke surmises, "My astonishment seems less an activity of mine, a willful projection of a function of my interests, than the deepest mode of passivity."[40] Vulnerability arises from such a surprise, a being caught off guard by the epiphany of the other person. My solitude is invaded by the other who seemingly comes from nowhere.

This element of "being caught off guard" is important here, because it indicates more about the presence of the other than the mere perception of the other. This catching off-guard makes me aware of the presence of the other as an other who is due my concern and has my attention at a deep level, not because I choose to give it to the other, but because it is demanded of me. In short, I want to consume the other, but cannot. Two steps involved in furthering this moment are proximity and substitution.[41] These two notions will lead us to an understanding of ethically missional

40. Burke, "Ethical Significance," 198.

41. It is important to note that Lévinas extends this distinction of proximity and substitution beyond his reflections in *Totality and Infinity* as he moves in *Otherwise than Being*.

responsibility in Lévinas, though it must be understood that responsibility is not derived from these steps; it is, rather, bound up with them.

Proximity and the Face

The face of the other, that element of the other that is the ground of interpersonal contact, is a direct immediacy with the other person that Lévinas calls "proximity."[42] Proximity is felt as immediate contact. Lévinas describes proximity in this way:

> The proximity of the Other is presented as the fact that the Other is not simply close to me in space, or close like a parent, but he approaches me essentially insofar as I feel myself—insofar as I am—responsible for him. It is a structure that in nowise resembles the intentional relation which in knowledge attaches us to the object—to no matter what object, be it a human object. Proximity does not revert to this intentionality; in particular it does not revert to the fact that the Other is known to me.[43]

The proximity of the other demands a response. In this way, Lévinas claims that proximity is responsibility, or the ability to respond.[44] Proximity must then be thought of as a weight upon me that comes from the outside. Unlike existential thinkers such as Jean Paul Sartre and Albert Camus, who find an antagonism in this entry of the other from the outside, Lévinas finds the possibility of ethics and meaning, or the ground upon which ethics first shows itself. Not only does the possibility of ethics show itself here, what it means to be a self now takes on a different characteristic. A new subjectivity is born that indicates that the self, in facing the other, findings a move of responsibility for the other. The very meaning of being a social self is to be for-the-other. For Lévinas, the fact remains—"Subjectivity is being hostage."[45] That is to say, this responsible

---

42. See Tallon, "Intentionality, Intersubjectivity," 304.

43 Lévinas, *Ethics and Infinity*, 96–97. "Proximity is not a state, a repose, but, a restlessness, null site, outside of the place of rest.... No site then, is ever sufficiently a proximity, like an embrace.... Proximity, as the 'closer and closer,' becomes the subject.... Proximity is the subject that approaches and consequently constitutes a relationship in which I participate as a term, but where I am more or less than a term." Lévinas, *Otherwise than Being*, 82.

44. See Lévinas, *Otherwise than Being*, 139: "Proximity, difference which is non-difference, is responsibility."

45. Ibid., 127.

self arises from confrontation with the other where the other is dominant, never reducible to the domain of the same. Subjectivity as responsible self in this vein means submission; my mission is found under the "that" of the other.

> The self is a sub-jectum: it is under the weight of the universe . . . the unity of the universe is not what my gaze embraces in its unity of apperception, but what is incumbent upon me from all sides, regards me, is my affair.[46]

The self is subjected to the other who comes from on high to intrude upon my solitude and interrupt my egoist enjoyment. The self, feeling the exterior in the guise of the other passing through its world, is already obligated to respond to the transcendent other who holds the self hostage. In turn, this means that "the latent birth of the subject occurs in an obligation where no commitment was made."[47] I do not agree to live ethically with the other at first, I am ordered to do so. The meaning of my being a self is found in opposition to the other, in an essential ability to respond to the other. In short, the economy or fullness of the other actually increases as I act ethically toward the other. The more just I am, the more obligated I am. The more I do for the other, the more I am required to do. I am, above all things, a social self *a priori*, summoned to stand in the place of the other.

Substitution and Standing in the Place of the Other

This standing in the place of the other provides Lévinas with one of his most powerful concepts in relation to our conversations toward a renewed sense of mission: "substitution." Substitution arises directly from the self as held in the necessary relationship to the other—I am incomplete without you. It is the means by which my being responds to the other before I know that it does. Indeed, substitution is a sign of how other-directed the human being actually is. In facing myself towards the other in substitution, my identity becomes concrete. "In substitution my being that belongs to me and not to another is undone, and it is through substitution that I am not 'another,' but me."[48] As Lévinas states succinctly in *Otherwise than*

---

46. Ibid.

47 Ibid., 140.

48. Ibid., 127.

Being, "the oneself cannot form itself, it is already formed with absolute passivity."[49]

What Lévinas proposes at this stage is that the depth-giving meaning of being a social subject is primarily to be for the other. The missional moment of substitution is a call of Jesus' model in Philippians 2 of *kenosis* as we outlined in the first chapter—a sacrifice of self, embracing the call of the kenotic self. If I am not willing to empty myself, and all that I grasp of my identity and sense of self, in order to truly encounter the face of the other, then I cannot truly have a relationship with the other. It is not enough to have merely the idea of being in the place of the other person, for ideas have yet to come on the scene. Alphonso Lingis in the introduction to *Otherwise than Being* puts it this way: "One is held to bear the burden of others: the substitution is a passive effect, which one does not succeed in converting into an active initiative or into one's own virtue."[50]

While it is true that Lévinas is vague on the notion of substitution, the suggestion seems to be that in being persecuted by the other, I am made to consider the other as a true other. However, since such consideration cannot be made on the conceptual level, this consideration becomes manifest in a placement of the self with full abandonment before the face of the other. Consideration for the other means being-considerate-for-the-other. Substitution then is recognizing myself in the place of the other, not with the force of a conceptual recognition, but in the sense of finding myself in the place of the other as a hostage for the other. Substitution is the conversion of my being as a subjection by the other into a subjection for the other.

In substitution Lévinas is also arguing for the ethical summons as that which is a primary connection between moral agents that is not in need of mediation. This is the difference between watching an act of violence on television and seeing an act of violence in person. In which case do you feel the greater summons to respond—the encounter that is mediated or the personal encounter? When the summons is brought forward, Lévinas says that at this moment the ethical command has been waged. You are obligated to respond. This is also true in mission encounters: if the desire to respond does not, at first, present itself as a command, and you respond because you want to respond, then you have just been witness

49. Ibid., 104–5.
50. Lingis, translator's introduction, xxxi.

to the depth that substitution has taken in your own being. The desire to respond is already a responsiveness to the command of the other.

Some ethicists find that if we respond to the person because we feel a personal need to do so, then we are really satisfying our own desire, and, as such, our action does not have true moral worth. Lévinas' point is more profound on this score. He notes that there is a metaphysical explanation for why we have this desire to respond. The explanation is rooted, once again, in substitution. First of all, the person has a transcendence that a television image of a person does not have, and secondly, we have, in fact, already substituted ourselves for the other. Within Lévinas' framework, the desire to help the other emerges because I am held hostage by the other to the core of my being, and, in substitution, I am made to stand for the other, before freedom and reason comes on the scene.

Substitution and Cormac McCarthy's The Crossing

To illustrate Lévinas' notion of substitution, I would like to offer a (re) reading from a section of Cormac McCarthy's novel *The Crossing*. McCarthy is an American novelist who has taken what many consider to be the most benign of literary genres—the American Western—and re-imagined it with a power that is nothing short of breathtaking. In this particular novel, set in barren borderlands of Texas and Mexico, a young boy comes upon the ruins of a village in the middle of the Mexican desert. All the homes have been burned out long ago, and in the middle of the village stands the ruins of a once impressive Catholic church. Nothing remains of the structure except for its large dome, which "hangs in the sky like an apparition,"[51] twisting and turning upon three huge columns that are all that remains of the nave. In the shadow of this haunting sight sits a solitary old man cooking upon a campfire. The boy comes to the man's fire and shares a cup of coffee amidst the creaking of the ever-moving dome above them. The man tells the boy that he is the custodian of this church, ruined though it may be. There is a story, he says, about this place, as there is a story about all places:

> Things separate from their stories have no meaning. They are only shapes. Of a certain size and color. A certain weight. When their meaning has become lost to us they no longer have even a name. The story on the other hand can never be lost from its place in the

51. McCarthy, *The Crossing*, 149.

world for it is that place. And that is what was to be found here
... the tale. And like all (places) it ultimately told one story only, for
there is only one to tell.[52]

This man tells the boy that he came to this place to retrace the steps
of a man who had lived long ago. It is important to know that this person's
story is our story, he says to the boy. "For this world ... which seems to us
a thing of stone and flower and blood is not a thing at all but is a tale. And
all in it is a tale and each tale the sum of all lesser tales and yet these also
are the selfsame tale and contain as well all else within them. So everything is necessary. Every least thing. This is the hard lesson."[53] With this,
the boy begins to hear the tale that is all tales found in this one person of
long ago.

> This particular man had come to this village of Caborca with his
> family. Here he was born and here he would ultimately die. His
> parents were killed by a cannon shot within the church as the vil-
> lage sought to defend itself against invaders. Amidst the ruins of
> this church that became a fortress and now a crypt for his family
> and village, the boy crawled free of the rubble and destruction and
> began to wander the land through the days of his youth and well
> into his manhood. Tragedy seemed to follow him all the days of
> his life until as a solitary pensioner he returned to the ruins of
> the once great church of Caborca which had been the place that
> had severed him from his history. The dome of the church hung
> against the sky from the time of his parent's death, twisting in the
> sun upon its uncertain three columns.
>
> No mason could devise such a structure. For years the people
> of Caborca waited for it to fall. It was like a thing unfinished in
> their lives. Events of doubtful outcome were made subject to its
> standing. It was said of certain old and venerable men that when
> they died the dome would fall and they died and their children
> died and the dome floated on in the pure air until at last it came to
> bear such import in the minds of the people of that town that they
> scarce would speak of it at all.
>
> This was what he came to. Perhaps he did not even consider the
> question as to how he had been brought to this place. Yet it was the
> very thing he sought. Beneath that perilous roof he threw down
> his pallet and made his fire and there he made ready to receive
> that which had eluded him. By whatever name. There in the ruins

52 Ibid., 142, 143.
53. Ibid., 143.

of that church out of whose dust and rubble he had been raised up seventy years before and sent forth to live his life. Such as it was. Such as it had become. Such as it would be.[54]

Slowly the people of the town came out to see what the man was doing and what would happen to him. None would go underneath the tormenting dome and all merely stood on the border and watched and listened. Eventually the village priest came out and urged him to come out, speaking "to this misguided man of the nature of God and of the spirit and the will and of the meaning of grace." The old man merely nodded and retorted, "you know nothing. That is what he shouted. You know nothing."[55] Each day the same thing—the people gathered to see what the priest, standing on the borders, would say to the man sitting amidst the shadow of this former place and present trauma.

> The old man at one point turned to the people, and the priest in particular, clearing his ancient throat, and said that both he and the priest were heretics—people who spoke and lived in relation to that which they knew nothing about.
>
> With this difference, he said. With this difference. The priest wagered nothing. He'd nothing at hazard. He stood on no such ground as the crazed old man. Under no such shadow. Rather he chose to stand outside the critical edifice of his own church and by this choice he sacrificed his words of their power to witness.[56]

The priest left and the villagers departed. The dome continued to sway and swagger for weeks upon weeks until the old man finally collapsed. The priest, overcoming his fear, came into shadows of the ruins and to the man's side, who whispered with one final breath, "As a man goes on a journey, save yourself." And with that he died.

The teller of this tale then turns to the young boy who has been sitting beside him and the campfire, which has been throwing shadows upon shadows of the same swaying dome mentioned throughout the tale. "The storyteller's task" he said, "is not so simple. You will have guessed by now of course who was the priest." With this he turns his face to boy and

---

54. Ibid., 150.
55. Ibid., 151.
56. Ibid., 152, 152.

says "To God every man is a heretic. The heretic's first act is to name his brother."[57]

An interesting ending to a rather apocalyptic tale. This story within a story that McCarthy tells is a "convicting" allegory of the safe role many choose in missional encounters in light of Lévinas' notion of substitution: As the priest turned custodian of ruins surmises, everyone is a heretic, and the heretic's first act is to name who their brother or sister is so that it is possible to be set free. In this way, it is encounter over and against disembodied reason that liberates and frees, or as we hear in 1 Corinthians 13, "for now we see in a mirror dimly, but then face to face. Now I know in part; then I shall understand fully, even as I have been fully understood."

One definition of heretic is one who is *sectarian*—completely partisan to one's own views and unwilling to understand the connection one has to another, that one is not unique in the questions one seeks. The salvific question before the heretic is one that Lévinas figures in his notion of substitution—the heretic's summons is a call of *le régard*, to abide within a gaze of the other. Unless there is substitution and a deep appreciation that all ask the same questions of ultimate concern, and all parts contribute to this effort, the search is doomed to failure. As McCarthy puts it, "the heretic's first act is to name his brother." In line with Lévinas, the heretic is summoned away from a sectarian life lived apart from others and therefore heeds the call to so intimately bind oneself to the story of the other that the stories—my story and the that of the other—become one.

The Kenotic Self as the Responsibility of the Face

This brings us, at last, to Lévinas' notion of ethical responsibility. This notion of responsibility, much in line with our concept of responsiveness, means that in being a subject I am already in the grip of the other. It also entails that all thought enters on the scene after the epiphany of the other in the face-to-face. This is to say that the other precedes my ethical subjectivity, and that ethics precedes any conceptual thought or science. Inasmuch as responsibility is foundational for all interpersonal relationships, it is in responsibility that we are going to find a means to pass from an encounter with the real other person into ethics. Lévinas writes,

> In [*Otherwise than Being*] I speak of responsibility as the essential, primary and fundamental mode of subjectivity. For I describe

57. Ibid., 158.

subjectivity in ethical terms. Ethics, here, does not supplement a preceding existential base [as Heidegger would have it]; the very node of the subjective is knotted in ethics understood as responsibility.[58]

Furthermore, "the tie with the other is knotted only as responsibility"[59] as well. Thus, responsibility is the link between the subject and the other person, or, in more general terms, the source of the moral "ought" is the appearance of the other person as a person instead of a thing. To say that responsibility is foundational for mission is to say then not only that responsibility is what relates one subject to another, but is to furthermore say that the meaning of the otherness of the other person is given in responsibility, not in my interpretation of the other person. The very meaning of being an other person is "the one to whom I am responsible." Thus, the contact with the real other person that I spoke of at the beginning as something presupposed by the very meaning of ethics turns out to be, in Lévinas' account, the source of the moral "ought."

Emptying of the Kenotic Self by the Summons of Others

In opposition to the notion of subjectivity that has dominated phenomenology since Husserl and even Hegel, Lévinas holds that subjectivity is not exhausted by its determination as consciousness—we are not lost in our encounter with the other. According to Lévinas, when philosophy (and for our discussion, the cultural formation of identity) takes the subject to be equivalent to consciousness, the very fact of being a subject is overlooked. "Consciousness already rests on a 'subjective condition,' an identity that one calls ego or I."[60] This subjective condition of the subject is what Lévinas calls the responsible self. As responsibility, the subjectivity of the subject means that, from the outset, I am subjected to the demands of the other—in other words, that from the moment I am, I am concerned not for myself but for the other. Within Lévinas' ethical understanding of subjectivity, the self no longer stands at the origin of any and all experience, as in a phenomenology of consciousness. What it means to be a self means that I come radically after the other, who calls me to responsibility before I am there. I am not my own origin since I am born in response

58. Lévinas, *Ethics and Infinity*, 95.

59. Ibid., 97.

60. Lévinas, *Otherwise than Being*, 102.

to the other: "signification as proximity is thus the latent birth of the subject. Latent birth for prior to an origin, an initiative."[61] Responsibility is therefore not an active engagement or commitment that a self undertakes at its own initiative, rather it is first assigned to its responsibility for the other. The responsible self is thus "compelled before commencing" in an essential and irreducible passivity.[62] Such a passivity, one that precedes the activity of the I or ego, cannot be interpreted in terms of a phenomenology of consciousness, where everything that befalls the self finds its origin in a possibility that consciousness constitutes beforehand, transcendentally for itself.

Since the subjective condition of the subject precedes and undoes consciousness, the self finds itself excluded from the field where knowledge and judgment are possible. The other who summons the subject therefore radically transcends language and knowing. The responsible self and the other cannot be coordinated within a common horizon, and terms other than those derived from knowledge and being are called for. This is a haunting and dangerous place for authentic identity to find a center point, but an authentic place nonetheless. For it is this liminal space—a thoroughly kenotic place of self-emptying ,where one is freed from the ability to totalise the other—that Lévinas summons those seeking community. This is a place that recalls Martin Heidegger's idea of *lichtung*—a clearing that is unfettered and clearly illuminated where the potential of *aletheia*[63] may indeed arise under ever deconstructing the temples of our own construction.

Insofar as responsibility describes the genesis of the subject prior to its being, responsibility must be described in terms of a Good beyond Being. Lévinas writes, "If ethical terms arise in our discourse . . . it is because . . . the subject finds himself committed to the Good in the very passivity of supporting."[64] This commitment to the Good, according to Lévinas, is the very genesis or birth of the subject in responsibility. "The Good choose[s] me first before I can be in a position to choose, that is,

61. Ibid., 139.

62. Ibid., 103.

63. Translated traditionally from the Greek as "truth", Heidegger employs the term more robustly as a neologism for "revealedness" and "unconcealedness." See Nussbaum, *Fragility of Goodness*, as well as Charles Guignon's editorial introduction *The Cambridge Companion to Heidegger*.

64. Ibid., 122.

welcome its choice. . . . The Good is before being."[65] In this way, the Good summons me before I am, before I have being, and it is in response to that summons that I am born as a responsible self. "The way I appear is as a summons."[66] In keeping with our discussion of the kenotic self, the relation between the Good as Lévinas describes it and the self whose origin it shapes is here described in terms of a summons, or call, which cannot be reduced to the relation between cause and effect or to any relation between two beings since the summons precedes and determines the eventual being of the other. This is a drama played out in deep responsibility and care that is not acted out merely by two beings, each seeking to pursue their own ends and to persevere in their own being, but in terms of goodness where the kenotic self gives up all that they could call their own in obedient response to the command of the hidden Good. Lévinas writes, "the self is goodness, or under the exigency for an abandon of all having. . . . Goodness invests me in my obedience to the hidden Good."[67] Like the created soul who is what it is in terms of the good it has received, the kenotic self as summoned for others exists only on account of its having received an investment of goodness which demands the dispossession of its own being in the proximity of the other.

From this summoned repose of the self we now look toward what it means to fully give—to release all that we have and hope to be—as the kenotic self in the movement of "theological givenness."

65. Ibid.
66. Ibid., 139.
67. Ibid., 118.

6

Forgetting the Kenotic Self through "Being Given"

The ministry of Jesus Christ is meaningless without reconciliation. The ministry of reconciliation is our collective commitment
to overcome the barriers that divide and alienate people from each
other by the healing power of love and unity that flows from the
Spirit of God. *The New Testament accounts of how Jesus ministered
at the margins of his society provide a strong foundation for teaching, modeling and promoting reconciliation both in the academy and
the church. . . . The ministry of reconciliation is fundamental to the
Christian faith. It is no accident that the Spirit chose an international, multi-cultural gathering of believers in Jerusalem as the setting
for the Pentecost outpouring, whose testimony was that "in our own
languages we hear them speaking about God's deeds of power" (Acts
2:11). Pentecost is God's remedy for disunity.* Many languages, many
colors, many cultures, but one testimony of one God.[1]

IN RELATION TO THE ethical and missional abandon called for in Derrida
and Lévinas in the previous chapter, let us continue this consideration
of a radically abandoned repose in the world as one that not only embodies a truthful openness that is the movement of the kenotic self before
the other, but does so out of a gospel-led response to God as one "being given." Here I am arguing for a revising of a non-essentialist notion
of God that provokes significant comparison to the work of Jean-Luc
Marion in *God without Being* as well as Marion's major work, *Being Given:
Toward a Phenomenology of Givenness.* As discussed in the introduction,
in the decade since the seminal revisioning of contemporary missiology
in works such as David J. Bosch's *Transforming Mission* (1991) through to
the current "The Gospel and Our Culture Series," which includes Darrell

1. Sanders, *Ministry at the Margins*, 92, 98.

L. Guder's *Missional Church* (1998) and George Hunsberger's *The Church between Gospel and Culture* (1996), much of missional methodology has lacked a critical philosophical assessment. In the previous chapter we reflected on the ways Continental philosophical thought provides methodological tools for both forming and grounding the self in a deep responsibility for the other. This is in keeping with the call of Jesus in the Great Commandment: "Love the Lord your God with all your heart, mind, soul and strength; and Love your neighbor as yourself." In this chapter we turn to the task of an authentic model of selfhood—what we have called the kenotic self—and seek how the forging of self for and with the other is also a call to "forget" oneself and "be given" through a sensitive and kerygmatic engagement in the world.

Our dialogue partner in this conversation will be philosopher Jean-Luc Marion. In Marion's reflection on the nature of God in book *God without Being*, he attempts to envisage, frame, and ultimately critique a notion of the divine seen in much of our culture into what he terms "Idol" as opposed to "Icon." As argued by Marion, the true icon does not result from a vision of the divine, but instead provokes one. Rather than resulting from the gaze aimed at it, the icon summons sight by allowing the invisible to saturate the visible, but without any attempt or claim of reducing the invisible to the visible icon. As argued by Marion, the true icon does not result from a vision of the divine, but instead provokes one. Rather than resulting from the gaze aimed at it, the icon summons sight by allowing the invisible to saturate the visible, but without any attempt or claim of reducing the invisible to the visible icon. In this way, Marion provides an intriguing challenge to our attempts to hold our sense of self in a static moment that remains in relation to the privileging of dogma over authentic kenotic encounters with the Living God. As will be discussed in the conclusion of this chapter, while other writers on mission have suggested a kenotic model for mission (such as Vincent Donovan in *Christianity Rediscovered*) Marion's priority to "givenness" as the qualitative aspect of authentic encounter between persons allows for a form of the kenotic self that is humble enough to see the potential of idolatry and the radical need for a deeply iconic understanding of openness in both our doctrine of God and various theologies of mission.

To exemplify the radical theological givenness called forth in Marion's modeling of God, I will reflect on the writing of Japanese author

Shusaku Endo[2] as illustrative of Marion's core contributions to a revised missional methodology and deep personhood.

Shusaku Endo's Silence and A Life of Jesus

Shusaku Endo's 1966 novel *Tinmoku* ("Silence") operates, as with most good art, on numerous levels. As a work of historical fiction, it successfully re-imagines the events of a sixteenth-century Portuguese priest in Tokugawa, Japan, named Rodrigues. As the narrative unfolds, the reader discovers that the most famous missionary in Japan, Father Ferreira, has apostatized. Father Rodrigues, who studied under Father Ferreira in seminary, cannot believe it possible that the great man would have renounced the faith after twenty years of courageous service. He sets sail to find Ferreira with the intention of discovering the truth—in all its manifest forms.

Rodrigues survives extreme hardship to reach Japan, and upon arrival he hears the confessions of secret Christians (members of the fledgling *Kakure* church) who have not seen a priest in years. It is a slow awakening to find that the form of Christianity Rodrigues experiences in Japan is not what he holds as orthodox. As surmised by the priest Ferreira at the end of the novel,

> "When you [missionaries] first came to this country churches were built everywhere, faith was fragrant like the fresh flowers of the morning, and many Japanese vied with one another to receive

2. While much has been written in literary criticism about Shusaku Endo's various historical and literary novels, particularly by William Johnston, SJ, and Van C. Gessel who have also served as key translators of Endo's works into English, this paper builds on their work and provides a necessary *theological* and *phenomenological* exploration of Endo's work. After studying Catholic literature and Continental philosophy in France in the early 1950s, Endo's literary work upon returning to Japan ranged from *Aden made* through to *Siroi Hito* ("A White Man") in *Kindai Bungaku*, *Umi to Dokuyaku* ("The Sea and Poison"), *Sikai no Hotori* ("Upon the Dead Sea") two essays on Jesus Christ, *Iesu no Shogai* ("A Life of Jesus) and *Kirisuto no Tanjo* ("Birth of Christ"), humorous work such as the *Korian* essays ("Neighbor of Old Fox" and "Raccoon Dog"), through to his last novel in 1973, *Fukai Kawa* "(Deep River"), where Endo explores religious pluralism and offers a theological reflection on reincarnation. Over the past decade there has been an increased awareness of Endo's literature in religious discourse, most recently seen in the Shusaku Endo panel formed for the 2003 American Academy of Religion conference. What is lacking is a sustained critical reflection of Endo's work in regard to his contribution toward a dynamic re-imagining of Christianity that is distinctly Eastern yet in conversation with Western themes and traditions.

baptism like the Jews who gathered at the Jordan. And suppos-
ing the God whom those Japanese believed in was not the God of
Christian teaching . . ." Ferreira murmured these words slowly, the
smile of pity still lingering on his lips . . .[3]

> The Japanese are not able to think of God completely divorced from
> man; the Japanese cannot think of an existence that transcends the
> human. . . . The Japanese imagine a beautiful, exalted man—and
> this they call God. They call by the name of God something which
> has the same existence as man. But that is not the Church's God.[4]

One of these Christians, Kichijiro, a shadowy and duplicitous fisher-
man akin to the biblical Judas, betrays Rodrigues' true identity as a priest
to the shogun in exchange for a reward. Rodrigues holds fast to the faith
he has brought with him to Japan even while under personal torture
and when faced with an unbearable moral situation involving groups of
Japanese Christians that are led to him to be tortured. He is told that if
he steps on the *fumie*, a bronze image of the face of Jesus, as a testimony
of his renouncing the Christian faith, they will be set free. He refuses,
and they are taken away and killed before his eyes. Rodrigues sees the
haunting face of Jesus numerous times throughout the narrative arch of
Silence—both figured in the various *fumie* images noted throughout the
novel as well as imagined in his dreams. This is a face he loves and serves;
but the face never speaks. It remains silent when the priest is chained to
a tree to watch the Christians die, silent when he asks for guidance on
whether to commit apostasy by stepping on the *fumie*, and silent when
he prays in his cell at night. One night Rodrigues hears a sound like snor-
ing—alluding to the sleeping disciples in Gethsemane—only to discover
that the sound is actually the tormented groans from Christians hanging
upside down over pits, their ears slit so that their blood will drip and they
die a slow, agonizing death. These, too, can be set free, if Rodrigues will
only recant.

Endo later complained that *Silence* was misinterpreted because of its
title. "People assume that God was silent," he said, "when in fact God does
speak in the novel." Silence is broken open when Rodrigues is contem-
plating the *fumie*:

> The priest raises his foot. In it he feels a dull, heavy pain. This is no
> mere formality. He will now trample on what he has considered

3. Endo, *Silence*, 225.
4. Ibid., 229.

the most beautiful thing in his life, on what he has believed most pure, on what is filled with the ideals and the dreams of man. How his foot aches! And then the Christ in bronze speaks to the priest:

"Trample! Trample! I more than anyone know of the pain in your foot. Trample! It was to be trampled on by men that I was born into this world. It was to share men's pain that I carried my cross." The priest placed his foot on the *fumie*. Dawn broke. And far in the distance the cock crew.[5]

Silence *as Theological Iconoclasm*

Endo locates the theme of the novel in the transformation of the face of Jesus, not the transformation of the characters. As Endo himself has stated, "To me the most meaningful thing in the novel is the change in the hero's image of Christ."[6] The image of Jesus that had appeared to Father Rodrigues numerous times is that of a transcendent, static heroic Jesus. Gradually, though, as Rodrigues's resolve to maintain this image of Christ as true faith, causing the death of many Japanese as a result—the face of Jesus begins to change into one marked by human suffering. At one point in the novel, Rodrigues gazes into his own reflection in a pool of rainwater:

There reflected in the water was a tired, hollow face. I don't know why, but at that moment I thought of the face of another man . . . the face of a crucified man . . . heavy with mud and with stubble; it was thin and dirty; it was the face of a haunted man, filled with uneasiness and exhaustion.[7]

From that point on, the novel uses words like suffering, uneasy, exhausted, and ugly to describe the face of Jesus. And when the silence finally breaks at the end of the novel, just as Rodrigues is about to step on the *fumie*, he recalls this face speaking to him:

The remembrance of that *fumie*, a burning image, remained behind his eyelids. The interpreter had placed before his feet a wooden plaque. On it was a copper plate on which a Japanese craftsman had engraved that man's face. Yet the face was different from that on which the priest had gazed so often in Portugal, in Rome, in

5. Ibid., 259.

6. Endo, quoted in Yancey, "Japan's Faithful Judas," 7.

7. Endo, *Silence*, 259.

Goa and in Macao. It was not a Christ whose face was filled with majesty and glory; neither was it a face made beautiful by endurance of pain; nor was it a face filled with the strength of a will that repelled temptation. The face of the man who then lay at his feet was sunken and utterly exhausted.[8]

A central concern in *Silence* and seen throughout Endo's writing is a contextual model for imaging a distinctive Japanese Christianity that transcends cultural idolatry. In his fiction, Endo puts forth a modeling of God that, while fictive in its poetic shape, finds philosophical and theological support and provokes significant comparison to the work of Jean-Luc Marion in *God without Being* and *Being Given: Toward a Phenomenology of Givenness*.

Jean Luc Marion—Idol and Icon

The question of transposing Jesus into a representational modality such as writing[9] has provoked countless theological and philosophical reflections. As Plato noted in *Phaedrus* in regard to when something moves into the realm of text,

> once a thing is put into writing, the composition drifts all over the place, getting into the hands not only of those who understand it, but equally of those who have no business with it; it doesn't know how to address the right people, and not address the wrong. And when it is ill-treated and unfairly abused it always needs its parent to come to its help.[10]

As argued by Marion in *God without Being*, attempts to envisage and frame notions of the divine provoke the forms of the idol and icon which typologically elicits a hermeneutic challenge akin to navigating Scylla and Charybdis. As Marion states at the beginning of *God without Being*,

8. Ibid., 264.

9. New Testament critic Stephen D. Moore aptly puts it this way: "As writing, Jesus must contend with invisible forces other than demons. As writing, he must be delivered up to powers other than the Jewish and Roman authorities. This force, this power, is the reader. Temma F. Berg asks: 'Who is the reader?' She replies: 'The reader is legion ("for we are many" –Mark 5:9). And to give oneself to readers, to allow strange others the power of breathing life into you, is to deliver yourself into the unknown. It is to take the greatest risk of all, the risk of annihilation, of death.' But if to write is to run the risk of death, it is also to seize the chance of life after death (undead, the author lives on in his or her tome) . . . writing also offers [Jesus] a body to live on in." Moore, *Mark and Luke*, 17, 18.

10. Plato, *Phaedrus*, 275.

For the historical succession of two models of "art" [the idol and
the icon] permits one to disclose a phenomenological conflict—a
conflict between two phenomenologies. The idol does not indicate,
any more than the icon, a particular being or even class of beings.
Icon and idol indicate a manner of being for beings, or at least for
some of them. Indeed, a determination that would limit itself to
opposing the "true God" (icon) to the "false gods," in extending the
polemic of the vetero-testamentary prophets, would not be suit-
able here.[11]

Marion goes on:

In short, the icon and the idol, are not at all determined as beings
against other beings, since the same beings (statues, names, etc.)
can pass from one rank to the other. The icon and the idol determine two manners of being for beings, not two classes of beings.[12]

For Marion, the idol presents itself to humanity's gaze (*le régard*)
attempting to represent the sacred and thus proposes to offer knowledge
pertaining to its otherwise invisible referent. It is the willingness of the
gaze to attribute such qualities to the idol rather than any quality of the
object itself which accounts for the object's status as Idol. For this reason
the gaze upon the idol proceeds no further once the idol is encountered
and further pursuit of the Sacred beyond the idol is stifled.] For Marion,
representations that draw and demand the gaze have the following
quality:

The idol fascinates and captivates the gaze precisely because everything in it must expose itself to the gaze, attract, fill, and hold it.
The domain where it reigns undividedly—the domain of the gaze,
hence of the gazeable [*régardable*]— suffices as well for reception:
it captivates the gaze only inasmuch as the gazeable comprises it.
The idol depends on the gaze that suffices that it satisfies, since if
the gaze did not desire to satisfy itself in the idol, the idol would
have no dignity for it.[13]

The demand of the idol as "the gaze's landing place"[14] is contrasted
with the icon:

11. Marion, *God without Being*, 7–8.

12. Ibid., 8.

13. Ibid., 10.

14. Ibid., 11. Thomas Carlson translates "[L]e point de *chute* du regard" as "the gaze's
falling-point" (emphasis mine).

> The gaze makes the idol, not the idol the gaze—which means that the idol with its visibility fills the intention of the gaze, which wants nothing other than to see. The gaze precedes the idol because an aim precedes and gives rise to that at which it aims. The first intention aims at the divine and the gaze strains itself to see the divine, to see it by taking it up into the field of the gazeable.[15]

The localizing of the gaze renders the fabrication of the sacred in the shape of the idol. As Marion puts it,

> [T]he fabricated thing exhausts the gaze and presupposes that this thing is itself exhausted in the gazeable. The decisive moment in the erection of an idol stems not from its fabrication, but from its investment as gazeable, as that which will fill a gaze. It dazzles with visibility only inasmuch as the gaze has drawn it whole into the gazeable and there exposes and exhausts it. The gaze alone makes the idol, as the ultimate function of the gazeable.[16]

In contrast to the idol, the true icon, as argued by Marion and illustrated in Endo's fiction, does not result from a vision of the divine, but instead provokes one. Rather than resulting from and being sustained by the gaze, the icon *summons* (*vocare*) sight by allowing the invisible to saturate the visible, but without any attempt or claim of reducing the invisible to the visible icon. This notion of "summons" brings us back to our discussion in the previous chapter with Lévinas and the summoned subject. The icon attempts to render visible the invisible as such, and ultimately (if we can use such essentialist rhetoric) shows nothing. It teaches the gaze to proceed beyond the visible into an infinity whereby something new of the invisible is encountered. As exemplified by Endo throughout his literature, the iconic gaze never rests or settles on the icon, but instead rebounds upon the visible into a gaze of the infinite.

In *Silence*, the summons of the icon comes from a number of destabilizing horizons of meaning that both reader and protagonist find difficult to reconcile and totalize. One aspect is the reconciliation of the beautiful and grotesque as qualitative aspects of Christ. As noted by Fumitaka Matsuoka, part of breaking through the *fumie* is the acknowledgment of the "grotesque" realm of life that is part of the incarnation in Endo's project:

15. Ibid.
16. Ibid., 10.

A life lived under the agony of personal failure and with the feeling of guilt and shame is what Endo calls the "grotesque" realm of life. Humans become open to what is beyond, for the grotesque touches upon the sacred. And the sacred reveals itself in the maternal image, even in the person of Jesus.[17]

Another challenge for the reader is the depicting of Christ as a maternal figure, thereby challenging gender essentialist understandings of Christology. Endo makes this point clear in the introduction to his *Iesu no Shogai* ("A Life of Jesus"):

> The religious mentality of the Japanese is—just as it was at the time when the people accepted Buddhism—responsive to one who "suffers with us" and who "allows for our weakness," but their mentality has little tolerance for any kind of transcendent being who judges humans harshly, then punishes them. In brief, the Japanese tend to seek in their gods and buddhas a warm-hearted mother rather than a stern father. With this fact always in mind I tried not so much to depict God in the father-image that tends to characterize Christianity, but rather to depict the kind-hearted maternal aspect of God revealed to us in the personality of Jesus.[18]

Rather than a distant transcendent figuring of Christ, Endo's maternal Jesus draws strong similarities to the Japanese notion of *dōhansha*—the constant companion. Mark B. Williams, in his book *Endo Shusaku: A Literature of Reconciliation*, sees this as a theme throughout his fiction:

> Here is Christ, the companion (*dōhansha*) figure so prominent in the author's work, a being who, resolved not to look down in judgment, chooses rather to share in the individual's pain and anguish as his "companion."[19]

Additionally, the nature of silence as the "voice" of God becomes a key theme throughout the novel. As the preist Rodrigues reflects,

> If God does not exist, how can man endure the monotony of the sea and its cruel lack of emotion? (But supposing . . . of course, supposing, I mean.) From the deepest core of my being yet another voice made itself heard in a whisper. Supposing God does not exist. . . .

17. Matsuoka, "Christology of Shusaku Endo."
18. Endo, *Life of Jesus*, 1.
19. Williams, *Endo Shusaku*, 122.

> This was a frightening fancy. If he does not exist, how absurd
> the whole thing becomes. . . . Plucking the grass as I went along
> I chewed it with my teeth, suppressing these thoughts that rose
> nauseatingly in my throat. I knew well, of course, that the greatest
> sin against God was despair; but the silence of God was something
> I could not fathom.[20]

Such a clash of opposites—the beautifully grotesque, the maternal
Christ, the silent voice—are what Thomas J. J. Altizer has argued as being
the essential character of a "true Christology," as calling forth a space that
evokes

> a full coming together of total opposites, the opposites of total
> ending and total beginning, and the totally old world or aeon and
> a totally new aeon or world . . . a *coincidentia oppositorum* is at
> the very center of the Christian epic, as is a calling forth and voy-
> age into an apocalyptic totality, and [the Christian] epic totality
> is an apocalyptic totality if only because it embodies such a radi-
> cal and total transformation. Here, this transformation is deepest
> in envisioning the depths of the Godhead itself, depths that are
> apocalyptic depths, and hence depths unveiling a new Godhead
> only by bringing an old Godhead to an end.[21]

For Altizer, to enter this parabolic enactment through the medium of
literature is to

> reverse every image of Jesus we have known if we are to be open
> to his contemporary and apocalyptic presence. Just such a reversal
> has continually occurred in the Christian imagination, a reversal
> not only of given images of Jesus, but also, and even thereby, a
> reversal of all given Christian images of God.[22]

From Fumie to Givenness

The move to the icon could be seen as merely a shift in conception
alone—a trading of one form of hubris for another. To his credit, Endo
remains a "priestly artist" rather than an "artistic priest" (one can think
of the important distinction set forth by Heidegger in his lectures on
Nietzsche and Hölderlin, where Heidegger sees Nietzsche as a *dichtender*

---

20. Endo, *Silence*, 105.

21. Altizer, *Contemporary Jesus*, xiv, xv, xxii, xiv.

22. Ibid., xxv.

Denker, "a poeticising thinker" in contrast to Hölderlin as the example of a *denkender Dichter*, "a thinking poet"). *Silence* does not fall into this trap and in doing so continues to remain a work of literature rather than a treatise for a revised Christology. As Salman Rushdie states in his essay "Is Nothing Sacred?,"

> Between religion and literature . . . there is a linguistically based dispute. But it is not a dispute of simple opposites. Because whereas religion seeks to privilege one language above all others, one set of values above all others, one text above all others, the novel has always been about the way in which different languages, values and narratives quarrel, and about the shifting relations between them, which are relations of power. The novel does not seek to establish a privileged language, but it insists upon the freedom to portray and analyze the struggle between the different contestants for such privileges.[23]

It is the freedom that Endo allows the different contestants for privileging that overturns not only the status of the fictive *fumie* as idol in the novel, but summons the gaze of the reader beyond the novel itself—the novel as idol—and *Silence* becomes an iconographic signifier for what Marion has termed "givenness."[24]

Silence provokes a constant tension in the visual-verbal intermeshing of signs. At one level, *Silence* is grafted to the biblical narrative notably through transposing and transforming the face of Jesus through the ironic trope of setting the image of Jesus into iconoclastic play of the various images that at once form and ultimately rupture—whether a bronze *fumie* of representation or a romantically re-imagined image in the mind as concept. This iconoclastic play of images that form and rupture challenges the essentialist repose in remembering the biblical Jesus as a dynamic not static directive framed in Luke 22:19, "do this in remembrance of me." Rendered from the Greek τοῦτο ποιεῖτε εἰς τὴν ἐμὴν ἀνάμνησιν,

---

23. Rushdie, "Is Nothing Sacred?" 102, 103.

24. By "iconographic signifier," I refer to Mieke Bal's definition as that which the artist utilizes to "help the reader recognize the preceding visual tradition, which in turn refers to the verbal text; in the second case the recognition is directly related to the text and works with the text's verbal devices. [We utilize] the term 'iconographic sign' for the sign that travels the visual-verbal route. The sign based upon the solely verbal reference then falls under the more encompassing concept of intertextuality and exemplifies the subcategory of pre-textual thematic reference." Bal, *Reading "Rembrandt"*, 184.

"do this" is from ποιεῖτε (*poiete*) from which the word "poetry" is derived.[25] This call of Jesus to "make poetic" is to make an imaginative leap into the memorial of Jesus' life and ministry in the truest sense of this Eucharistic command so that the people of God may find freedom beyond idolatry. Where does the gaze find its freedom? In *Being Given*, Marion explores that which gives rise to the phenomena that forms/takes form as idol and icon—what Marion terms "givenness." It is this notion of givenness that I now wish to explore, and in particular, how Endo's *Silence* evokes what I have termed *theological givenness*—which is the liberative enactment of givenness embodied in iconic theological poetics. In this way, theological givenness provides the role of midwife to the gaze that is being summoned through and beyond theology *qua* theology to that which gives itself as givenness.

Marion and Givenness

Drawing from the phenomenological tradition of Husserl and Heiddegger, Marion makes the following observation:

> In all science—therefore in metaphysics—it is a question of proving. To prove consists in grounding appearances in order to know with certainty, leading them back to the ground in order to lead them to certainty. But in phenomenology—that is to say, at least in what it intends, in the attempt to think in a nonmetaphyscial mode—it is a question of showing. To show implies letting appearances appear in such a way that they accomplish their own apparition, so as to be received exactly as they give themselves.[26]

Marion places great emphasis on moving beyond the traditional aspect of phenomenological reduction seen in the legacy of Husserl that strives to bracket the phenomena and thereby reduce the field of inquiry to the phenomena at hand:

> If in the realm of metaphysics it is a question of proving, in the phenomenological realm it is not a question of simply showing (since in this case apparition could still be the object of a gaze, therefore a mere appearance), but rather of letting apparition show *itself* in its appearance according to its appearing. The mere transi-

---

25. See Keuss, *Poetics of Jesus*, 205.

26. Marion, *Being Given*, 7.

tion from proving to showing therefore does not yet modify the deep status of phenomenology, nor does it assure it its freedom.[27]

Marion goes on to say that

> The movement from showing to letting *itself* show, from manifestation to self-manifestation starting from the self of what shows its *self*. But letting apparition show *its self* in the appearance and appearing as its own manifestation—that is not so self-evident. For a fundamental reason: because knowledge always comes from me, manifestation is never evident by itself. Or rather, it is not so self-evident that it can run its own course, coming from itself, through itself, starting from itself, in short, that it can itself manifest its *self*.[28]

In this regard,

> Phenomenological method therefore claims to deploy a turn, which goes not simply from proving to showing, but from showing in the way that an *ego* makes an object evident to letting an apparition in an appearance show *itself*: a method of turning that turns against itself and consists in this reversal itself—counter-method.[29]

The temptation to replace method with the *döppelganger* of counter-method is demonstrated in *Silence* in the visage of the Interpreter. Typologically tied to the role of Satan in Jesus' temptation in the desert, the Interpreter (one could say "the Hermeneut") continually presses Rodrigues to separate *theoria* from *praxis*—the ideal of faith in Jesus and the act of stepping on the *fumie*:

> "It is only a formality. What do formalities matter?" The interpreter urges him on excitedly. "Only go through with the exterior form of trampling."[30]

While the Interpreter attempts to convince Rodrigues that *theoria* and *praxis* can be kept to separate domains, the reader observes the foolishness of such a proposition:

> Slowly there appeared on the faces of the watching official's faint smiles. What had caught their attention was not the actual fact of

27. Ibid., 8; emphasis added.
28. Ibid., 8–9; emphasis added.
29. Ibid., 10; emphasis added.
30. Endo, *Silence*, 259.

the Christians placing their foot on the *fumie* but the expressions on their faces as they did so.

"You think you can deceive us like that?" said one of the officials, an old man. And now for the first time the three recognized him as the old samurai who'd ridden into Tomogi some days before. "Do you think we are fools? Do you think we didn't notice how heavy and nervous your breathing became . . ."[31]

In a similar fashion, one can choose a counter method by merely substituting terms/signs and never approach the signifier, that which Victorian novelist George Eliot called the "mystery beneath the processes." As Marion states in relation to Heidegger,

> Just as givenness is substituted for the Being that it brings to light better than it ever could itself—what Heidegger himself just showed—so too does the *Ereignis* [event horizon] also substitute itself for the "it" of the "it gives," therefore also for givenness. This so-called greater light is therefore obscuring. It hides, by the advent of the advent, Being (which remains coherent with the project) as well as givenness (which contradicts the project). Heidegger will admit as much elsewhere: "The gift of presence is the property of the Advent [*Eigentum des Ereignens*]. Being vanishes in the advent [*verschwindet im Ereignis*]."[32]

In contrast to this, Marion puts forward the *via media* through method and counter-method as givenness:

> Givenness often gives the given without measure, but the gifted always keeps within its limits. By excess or by default, givenness must in many cases renounce appearing—be restricted to abandon. Phenomenality always admits limits, precisely because givenness, which transgresses them, gives itself over only to my finitude.[33]

In a true phenomenological repose, Marion finds deep meaning as givenness[34] that unfolds and overturns categorical framing.

> The phenomenon shows itself inasmuch as it unfolds in it the fold of givenness; it always keeps, at the end of this unfolding, the mark of the passage, trajectory, or movement that it accomplished in

31. Ibid., 58.

32. Marion, *Being Given*, 37.

33. Ibid., 319.

34. Later Marion will expand this discussion into his reflections on *saturated phenomena* in *In Excess: Studies of Saturated Phenomena*, esp. 1–30.

order to come forward. The given testifies, by the trembling with which it still and always vibrates, not only to its irreversible and intrinsic difference, but also to its incessantly lost and repeated happening. It therefore attests that if it appears (shows itself) it owes this only to itself, only to its *self* (which gives itself).[35]

This is the ultimate depth of the face that beholds and speaks as Silence—both *as* the novel and throughout Endo's novel. Endo challenges readers to retract their gaze that has resided upon the supposed protagonist Father Rodrigues and instead look beyond toward the summoning silence that is shifting and ever-rupturing givenness—the true protagonist of the story.[36] As theological givenness, Christ is afforded the self-freedom to "be given" and not reduced or framed. This destabilizing *coincidentia oppositorum* is a decentering center in which Rodrigues is placed, as is the reader, since

> at the center stands no "subject," but a gifted, he whose function consists in receiving what is immeasurably given to him, and whose privilege is confined to the fact that he is himself received from what he receives.[37]

As Heidegger has aptly stated, *Wo die Theologie aufkommt, [hat] der Gott schon die Flucht begonnen* ("Wherever theology comes up, God has been on the run for quite a while").[38] It is in true fiction[39] such as Shusaku Endo's *Silence* that the possibility for the kenotic self is truly seen as mov-

35. Marion, *Being Given*, 321.

36. The end of *Silence* has Father Rodrigues recede to a shadowed figure only glimpsed at through two different reports akin to Gospels. As noted by Mark B. Williams, "The intervening years provide invaluable scope for Endō's narrator to adopt a objective perspective in his portrayal of the protagonist [Christ], . . . Much of the time is occupied in writing a '*shomotsu*' (lit. book, documents) and, in view of the fact that Rodrigues is writing this 'at the command of Tōtōminokami' it is clear that the *shomotsu* on which he is engaged represents more than a work he is compiling out of interest or to wile away the time. . . . Even now, some twenty years after his initial apostasy, Rodrigues is still vacillating; the desire to remain faithful to his creed remains in conflict with acknowledgement of the need to adopt a more pragmatic approach towards the authorities." Williams, *Endo Shusaku*, 117.

37. Marion, *Being Given*, 322.

38. Heidegger, quoted in Schäfer, "The Sacred."

39. "In other words, the writers of the Gospels were not following the necessities of history, the critical examination of evidence, the sifting, the winnowing, the interrogation, the torture of witnesses. They were following the necessities of the religious imagination, as that imagination had been trained by a millennium of poetry to imagine." Templeton, *New Testament*, 37.

ing beyond the idol-held gaze and responding to the summons of theological givenness, which fulfills the injunction evoked by the words "do this in remembrance of me."

PART TWO

The Space of the Self

7

The Kenotic Self and Missional Openness

... the goal of all Christian community: they meet one another as bringers of the message of salvation. As such, God permits them to meet together and gives them community. Their fellowship is founded solely upon Jesus Christ and this "alien righteousness." All we can say, therefore, is: the community of Christians springs solely from the Biblical message of the justification of man through grace alone; this alone is the basis of the longing of Christians for one another. Second, a Christian comes to others only through Jesus Christ. . . . Without Christ there is discord between God and man and between man and man. Christ becomes the Mediator and made peace with God and among men. Without Christ we should not know God, we could not call upon Him, nor come to Him. But without Christ we also would not know our brother [or sister], nor could we come to him [or her]. The way is blocked by own ego. Christ opened up the way to God and to our brother [and sister]. Now Christians can live with one another in peace; they can love and serve one another; they can become one. But they can continue to do so only by way of Jesus Christ. Only in Jesus Christ are we one, only through him are we bound together. To eternity he remains the one Mediator. . . . Our community with one another consists solely in what Christ has done to both of us. . . . I have community with others and I shall continue to have it only through Jesus Christ. The more genuine and the deeper our community becomes, the more everything else between us recede, the more clearly and purely will Jesus Christ and his work become the one and only thing that is vital between us. We have one another only through Christ, but through Christ we do have one another, wholly, and for all eternity.[1]

---

1. Bonhoeffer, *Life Together*, 23, 25–26.

THIS CHAPTER WILL EXPLORE how a mission of openness will methodologically refigure and re-imagine the theological categories of
Christian tradition and contemporary context for the kenotic self. As noted by theologian C. S. Song's discussion of Asian theological models in his
Third Eye Theology, the "third eye" of theology, a term derived from Zen
Buddhism and the Kyoto School, is the perspective of seeing Christ with
one's cultural experience and oneself as another. As Song describes this,
we must engage in an open dialogue with the world around us. For Song,
this occurs by juxtaposing Asian stories (representation of truth) with
biblical stories (content of abiding truth), and interprets the Asian stories
in correspondence with Christian theologies. The juxtaposition as such
is the methodology for implementing the "contextualization of theology,"
whereby "God images God's own self in humanity. . . . By imaging God's
own self in humankind, God imparts to us the ability to image all created
things in relation to God. God has giving us the power of theo-logical
imaging."[2] As we saw in the last chapter, this is exemplified by Japanese
novelist Shusaku Endo where the writing of fiction as "third eye" theological imaging radicalizes Song's project with a contextually grounded
yet fully imaginative account of the life of Jesus. As will be discussed in
this chapter, our "third eye" needs to be both fixed and reframed on the
dynamic nature of the person of God—which we will assert is "missionally open" to the world and therefore transforms our identity from a fixed
sense of personhood over and against the world to a deep and intimate
summons by the other.

Clark Pinnock and The Openness of God

The phrase "openness of God" is a theological model for the doctrine of
God that is aligned with what is called free-will theism. This is a view of
the doctrine of God that seeks to correct what is seen as an overly im-
mobile view of God wherein the Divine is unmoving and unchanging to
the point of being unable to respond or even love. For theologians such as
Pinnock, the "open" view of the doctrine of God sees God as compassionate in keeping with the character of the Divine as seen in the ministry of
Jesus and the outpouring of the Holy Spirit, in favor of a more cooperative
relationship between God and humanity in the healing of our world. The
use of the term "openness" by these writers underscores the conviction

2. Song, *Third Eye Theology*, 63.

that God is open to that which is created and therefore not distant and unaffected by the pain and suffering in creation. As suggested by Clark Pinnock and others, this stands in contrast to traditions that deny that anything outside God can impact God.[3]

According to Pinnock, the open view is in part a theological model that serves as a shorthand for expressing the simple fact that God is indeed complex. For Pinnock, instead of portraying God as an all-determining monarch or a completely unchanging substance, the open view understands God as a personal, relational, loving, triune Subject.

Open theism therefore an attempt to find a viable middle way—a *via media*—between classical theism and the dynamism of Process thought.[4] Pinnock has called the project of open theism simply "the appeal for a metaphysics of love, grounded in the gospel."[5]

Missiological Openness: The Challenge of the Open View of God to Cultural Identity Formation

It should be noted that much of the controversy surrounding the open view of God has resided in the evangelical portion of the church, especially in North America. Theologians in mainline denominations as well as Catholic and Eastern theologians have written little on the issue. As Pinnock and others supporting open theism have noted, it is ironic that the tension over open theism has existed primarily within evangelicalism, which is a movement without a central confessional statement but with strong theological interests and a generally conservative ethos. An evangelical theologian in this sense can be expected to hold to sound doctrines and contend for the faith delivered to the saints, though in a transdenominational way reflecting a rather broad coalition. In the perspective of postconservative evangelicals, who are carrying on the reform of fundamentalism, theological rethinking is part of a search for a generous orthodoxy and a more effective church and worldwide witness.[6]

---

3. See Tiessen, *Providence and Prayer*, chs. 4–5; see also Pinnock et al., *Openness of God*.

4. Feinberg, *No One Like Him*, 62–73.

5. See Hall and Sanders, *Divine Debates*. Books in favor of open theism include Pinnock, *Most Moved Mover*; Sanders, *God Who Risks*; and Boyd, *God of the Possible*. Books opposed to open theism from evangelicals include Ware, *God's Lesser Glory*; Frame, *No Other God*; and Geisler and House, *Battle for God*.

6. See Pinnock, "Evangelical Theology in Progress."

In counterpoint to open theism's movement toward a robust, dynamic doctrine of God, the movement of the kenotic self as we have seen in the previous chapters is a calling forth to be radically decentered (after Derrida and Lévinas) into a robust, dynamic movement of deep identity. Drawing in our discussions with missional and emergent voices, this movement of deep identity is also a call to become "openly missional" as a self, which reforms not only how we understand the very important doctrine of God, but also how we share this dynamic loving God to the world. In Pinnock's writing he has noted that theological patriarchs such as Irenaeus, Augustine, and Thomas Aquinas have taken similar dynamic views of the doctrine of God in relation to personhood. Key attributes of God's immutability, eternality, and sovereignty are more dynamic in many patriarchal writers than some twentieth-century interpreters report. As Pinnock has noted in *The Openness of God*, "open theists" are certainly not the only ones doing such reconsideration, and it is time that contemporary missiologists and others working on the question of theological anthropology and identity formation step forward as well. This call for fresh proposals for our concept of personhood, according to Pinnock, should be made in light of new conversation partners that are passionate about following the Spirit's leading when it concerns the nature of God and the proclamation of the gospel. Part of the hope in this chapter is to bring Continental thinkers such as Derrida, Lévinas, and Marion, introduced in the previous chapters, into this discussion on the doctrine of God, as Pinnock suggests, so that these new conversation partners may help both revision the depth of our humanity accomplish a dynamic reappropriation of the God who kenotically calls us into live abundantly.

This call toward dynamic movement and depth found in the nexus of a kenotic self and the doctrine of God finds its headwaters in the Scriptures. As we hear, the Good News is without limit, deep and inexhaustible, where "the depth of the riches and wisdom and knowledge of God" (Rom 11:33) are coupled with "the love of Christ that surpasses knowledge" (Eph 3:19). The call of the gospel is an inexhaustible mystery, and the ways of responding to God are innumerable. Though we "look through a glass darkly" and "know only in part," the vocation of the gospel provokes us toward willing and open repose of cooperation and generosity (1 Cor 13:12) with new voices seeking after truth, yet always in submission to the gospel it seeks to fulfill.

As made clear in his developed doctrine of the Holy Spirit entitled *Flame of Love*, Pinnock states that growing deeper in wisdom through the word of God as deep identity formation is made possible through the movement and continued work of the Holy Spirit. On the one hand, the Spirit binds us to the definitive salvific action of God in Jesus Christ, and on the other hand, causes everything that Jesus said and did to be seen in a new light. As made clear in John's Gospel, the *paraclete* guides the community into ever deepening truth (and unconcealedness to recall Heidegger's *aletheia*). This ever deepening call toward truth in the Spirit does not add to or surpass what Christ has revealed but causes everything to be seen afresh in our age.

The journey of the kenotic self is a willingness and courage to open ourselves afresh to Scripture and listen with the community to what the Spirit is saying to the churches about how to do mission, what the mission field is, and (as the focus of this book has attested to) what and where is the source of authentic identity to be found in our culture today. As Pinnock has noted in his work, theology is ultimately an unfinished task and must not become abstract speculation buried in a labyrinth of academic triviality. It is meant to keep the church faithful to the revelation of God and to make sure that she witnesses to Jesus Christ as a living reality in today's world.

The Kenotic Self as Missional Openness

What is the impact upon identity development from this vantage point of the doctrine of God? What I am calling "missional openness" is a relational missional model that asks (1) how our understanding of personhood is changed as our doctrine of God is more dynamic, and (2) how our understanding of mission would be affected if we believed that God, for the sake of love, had given human creatures libertarian freedom. To further our discussion of Kenosis in the opening chapter, what if we take seriously the vocational mandate of Philippians 2 and live accordingly with God, who restrained all power both human and divine so that the creation might exist as a significant other and be bound fully to purposeful intimacy rather than objectivity? Missional openness lifts up the Living God, whose very being is self-giving love and who is prepared to be vulnerable in his engagement with the world.

This call of missional openness, which I am asserting as the purpose and movement of the kenotic self, involves embracing rather than merely thinking of God as essentially loving and essentially relational.[7] As we have discussed in the preceding chapters in relation to Continental philosophies, the radical view of personhood as the kenotic self is constructed by both internal (Augustine) and external (Aristotle) concerns, radically decentered in location (Derrida), found in the face of the other (Lévinas), and "given" rather than taken (Marion). As we now turn to the model of the *imago Dei*—the image of God as the core of our identity—we realize that we are therefore formed akin to the Trinity whose concern is complete kenotic (self-emptying) love and does not just commit to love from afar. God as Father, Son, and Spirit is a triune personal communion of love which shares its own life and glory with human creatures and calls all to this "divine dance" or *periochoresis*. As the kenotic self is contextualized in the world as missional openness, the self sees God—Father, Son, and Holy Spirit—as both changing and unchanging, as suffering and not suffering, as temporal and supra-temporal. Akin to the heart of Arminian thought, it accepts self-restraint in God as a move of deep power rather than weakness, which makes room for us and which sees the triune God opening space for the sake of love. It sees God's sovereignty as an ever increasing realm of mercy and grace radically open to manifold means of drawing lovers to the Beloved. As a reformed theologian, I also see this move of missional openness as a deeper reading of Calvinism to its very core. Some reformed theologians underscore the primary orienting concern for God's sovereignty as complete control without room for human dignity to freely reciprocate love to its creator. The kenotic self holds that God's sovereignty is beyond our understandings of "control" and as such upholds God's self-limitation in kenosis (Philippians 2), thereby bestowing full agency and dignity to humanity through this radical self-limiting sovereignty.

In this regard, the kenotic self as missionally open is a repose in the world that holds its ever forming form in reference to the deeply real embodiment of God's love. In other words, to embody the kenotic self is to humbly seek the counterpoint of that *imago Dei* in the face of the other.

---

7. The notion of the Social Trinity is not new to theological discussion. Drawing from Eastern theological models of the doctrine of God such as in Zizoulas's *Being as Communion*, the Social Trinity model begins with the affirmation of the Godhead as relational prior to singularity.

This veers away from an abstract and impersonal approach to Divine mystery in favor of interactive, relational, and personal categories. As noted by Pinnock in *Most Moved Mover*, classical theism's root metaphor is God as a stone pillar around which everything else moves, which renders impossible real personal relations between God and humanity. The kenotic self as missionally open begins with the root image of a living personal triune God whose self-releasing and self-relinquishing act of kenosis empowers loving relations with humanity most clearly seen in the incarnation. In light of missional openness, the kenotic self sees the sovereign God allowing humanity to experience mutual and reciprocal relations of love within the fullness of the Godhead and with fellow creatures. For the purposes and fullness of love, God allowed some of his actions to be conjoined with our prayers and responses to God's call. God elicits our collaboration in his plans and has decided not to control everything but leave room for us to operate. This means that God exercises creative rather than restrictive sovereignty in dealing with us. Rather than some missional methodologies that overly utilize the human sciences to determine the approach of the data set known as the human condition, missional openness begins with the authority of Scripture, canonically centered and forever formed under the guidance of the triune God expressed in tradition and revelation. God (Father, Son and Spirit) is eternally giving and receiving love. This is not a philosophical structure bound to reason but a Trinitarian understanding that lifts up the heart of the gospel and projects a vision of God's graciously relational nature. The kenotic self sees God, in love and by sovereign power, creating the world out of nothing, yet forming creatures capable of experiencing divine love. To this end, God gave humans the capacity to enter into relationships with God and fellow creatures by granting them the freedom necessary for such relationships. And, despite the fact that we abuse our freedom by turning away from God, God remains faithful to his intentions for us.

The triune God is not a solitary monad but self-communicating love, not a supreme will to power as Nietzsche proposed but the will to and for salvation and continued animation of all there is. God, for the kenotic self, is the ultimate power whose very being consists in the giving, receiving, and sharing of love in and with the kenotic outpouring and release of the incarnation. In this way, to worship God is not to align ourselves with absolute power, infinite egocentrism, or majestic solitariness, but creative, sacrificial, and empowering love, whose glory consists not in dominating others but in sharing life with them. Such love is precarious, involves vulnerability, and gives us the dignity to return that love freely and openly.

Kenosis as the Missiological Method of God

In reference to the opening chapters, one way to understand the kenotic self as missional openness is to think of it as the kerygmatic echo of God's self-emptying and therefore the fulfillment and zenith of our life in and with God. As has been argued throughout this book thus far, the theological importance of kenosis has deep implications for a dynamic notion of personhood in respect to the dynamic openness of God.[8] Not only does it express the notion of the Son of God surrendering divine glory in order to become human, of his choosing to enter fully into the creaturely condition, and even share in our suffering, it also points to the divine mystery underlying it: that God wants to be loved by us and willingly makes himself vulnerable. Though we are completely dependent on him, God is also willing to be dependent on us. The kenotic self therefore sees God's self-giving and self-sacrificing action for the good of others pre-eminently in Jesus Christ, who is the image and self-expression of the Father (Heb 1:3). It is characteristic of love to be self-sacrificing, and the incarnation reveals to us so strongly how God likes to use his power not to dominate, but to love.[9]

This Divine self-emptying, in which God limits the exercise of his properties in order that significant creatures should exist, is also balanced by a pleroma, or extreme fullness, in which God experiences gain and not only diminishment. The act of self-emptying allows God to experience loving relationships with creatures that would otherwise have been impossible. We need to see that, alongside what looks like subtraction and loss, there is addition and gain, namely, the richness added to divine experience by enjoying these relationships. The self-limitation of God makes possible and renders visible new forms of Divine glory. In this regard the kenotic self does not serve a diminished deity akin to the emphasis of neo-paganism discussed in chapter 4. Unlike the anxiety around conservation and preservation that surrounds the neo-pagan view of the divine,

---

8. Feenstra, "Reconsidering Kenotic Theology."

9. Arminius underscores the need to emphasize God's self-limitation. Reformed theologians have acknowledged condescension in God's revelation. See Muller, *God, Creation*, 281.

in this there is no worry that we will somehow exhaust God, since it is only a question of how God's power and overflowing sustenance, which is his alone, is exercised.

As evidenced throughout Scripture, God chooses self-limitation for the sake of having a covenant with humankind and all creation. Rather, God in the gospel of Jesus Christ is completely aware of the finite world and intimately involved in the flow of events—God is God of time as well as the timeless. God is the key participant in the history of the world. God relates with us in temporal ways and experiences events as they occur. In creating the world, there took place a *kenosis* of omnipotence in which God allowed a created order to exist alongside the fullness of the Trinity and let it function so that, while all that happens is permitted by God, not all that happens in it is in accordance with the will of God.

In alignment with our reading of Lévinas in chapter 5, God does not employ the kind of power that annihilates the other in homogeneity, but rather steps back and allows otherness to be.

As for Divine eternality, the kenotic self in the context of missional openness holds that God is temporal in our context and works in time with us. As Pinnock and others have argued amidst the open theism discussions, timelessness needs to be re-imagined in light of our deeper understandings of time, especially after quantum theory and superstring theory. By bringing into being a temporal creation, whose nature is expressed in its unfolding history, God granted reality to time and actualized in his own nature through time. God is involved with time and history, indicating that there is in God both that which is wholly free from variation (so that God's character is eternally unchangeable) but also that which corresponds to the changing circumstances of a temporal creation. The eternal God can embrace the experiences of time and, as the incarnation and salvation history shows, it is not something foreign to him. God exists throughout all periods of time and is always our contemporary.[10]

Therefore, the kenotic self formed with a heart of missional openness takes a very bold stand when it comes to the foreknowledge of God. Missional openness takes Scripture seriously when it speaks of God's being open to the events and movements of humanity (Isa 5:4). God knows all that can be known but, because he is engaged with history, does not know all that will eventually be known. If God's project is dynamic and

10. See Feinberg, *No One Like Him*, 427–33, and "Unqualified Divine Temporality."

the future is open to what creatures (as well as God) will decide to do, then the future is not yet fixed and is not to be exhaustively foreknown. This does not imply that God is unprepared for any possible future or that God lacks the competence to face it. God knows all possibilities, but not yet as actualities. This is not only biblically sound and intellectually satisfying, but immensely practical. If God knows everything that will happen in the future, what is the point of petitionary prayer? The kenotic self in a stance of missional openness for the sake of creation holds that the triune God does not have exhaustive definite foreknowledge of every detail of the future, but has so arranged things that the future will be created through Divine-creaturely interaction. In terms of sovereignty, it means that God exercises general rather than meticulous providence and leaves the future for us to participate fully in.

Lastly, the kenotic self affirms God's omnipotence and omniscience. Standing the midst of the embracing Trinity poured out of all but love, the kenotic self as missionally open in and for the world attempts to move deeper than disagreements that distract our collective witness over whether God is fully omnipotent and omniscient, while matters for legitimate discussion need to be subjected to deeper and more missionally focused issues. Though self-sufficient in glory and lacking in nothing, God nevertheless makes room for creatures and deploys his power on their behalf, not against them. In the name of love, God self-limits and even self-sacrifices. If God had only love without power (as in process theism), God would be a compassionate but indifferent spectator of the world, as the deist asserts. If God had only power without love (as in deterministic theologies), God would be a cosmic tyrant without mercy or grace. In contrast, the triune God is neither an idle bystander nor a divine puppet master. God is love and deploys power for the good of humanity. God even permits the wayward freedom of his creatures and enters into their pain. The history of the world is the movement from divine self-emptying to our creaturely fulfillment in God. The kenotic self in the context of missional openness rejoices in this understanding, which proclaims that God is a free and creative triune personal God.

Having discussed the formative context of the kenotic self, which we have framed in part 1 as the "movement" of the kenotic self, we will now transition to more pragmatic discussions of ways in which living out an identity formed through otherness, givenness, and self-emptying for the sake of Christ's gospel—what we will term the "space" of the kenotic self in part 2. Here we will address the role that economics, urban life, and the form of worship as sacramental provide examples for how we live out our calling as the kenotic self in and for the world.

8

The Kenotic Self and Emergently Responsive Economics

T‍HE CALL OF MISSIONAL openness is a call to authentic missional responsiveness in and for the world that occupies the heart of God. This needs to be not only a call on the abstracted community of believers, but a strong pull on the very heart of the kenotic self. The fact that we need a better understanding of economics in relation to how the Christian faith encounters the world in which we live should come as no surprise. The traditional metrics of wealth and poverty have been found wanting, and the current upheaval in relation to the ever growing rift between the haves and the have-nots is not slowing. In short, something has got to give. The church's call to witness is continually compromised as it forgoes embracing this important tension that effects every living person on the planet—how do we (as the body of Christ) embody a responsive economic repose in the world that moves beyond rhetoric and into praxis that reflects the call of Philippians 2, emptying ourselves and taking the form of servants?

Postmodernism and "the New Poverty"
—"that which has ceased to be . . ."

As Carl Raschke has pointed out in his book *The Next Reformation*,[1] postmodernism has raised, not lowered, the bar for the body of Christ as to what "form" our collective lives should take. Some have been dismissive as to the role postmodern critique can bring to the current questions brought forward with "the new poverty." Comments that see postmodern critique as merely "intellectual Velcro dragged across culture," which "can

---

1. Raschke, *Next Reformation*.

be used to characterize almost anything one approves or disapproves,"[2] or as Umberto Eco quipped, "it is applied today to anything the users of the term happen to like."[3] American evangelicalism has been reticent to utilize the tools of postmodern critique to retrofit the gospel for the *zeitgeist* and, in the end, has only reinforced systems of economic slavery in the name of gospel and whispered as "the prayer of Jabez."

This Kuhnian paradigm shift in the Western philosophical tradition called "postmodernism" has made ready our culture for encountering the challenge of "the new poverty"—poverty that is not measured solely by conventional economic indicators such as GNP or cost-of-living indexes, but a deeper understanding of "poverty" that has financial uncertainty as the symptom to a deeper spiritual and psychic crisis in our time that includes loss of hope, lack of support, and gross marginality of people groups. This is the "new" poverty in so much as it is the same old poverty made new in our time—the deep poverty that Jesus spoke of when we turn our back on God and neighbor is even harder to acknowledge today after a century of unbridled capitalism has successfully numbed our culture to the holistic questions of body, mind, soul, and strength.

Daniel Adams made this point clear. "It is obvious that modernism as an ideology of Western culture is in serious trouble. At the present time, however, no one knows for certain what will arise to take modernism's place. The post-modern is the name given to this space between what was and what is yet to be."[4]

As we attempt to frame the global aspects of a new measure for poverty and grounded economic reflection, it is helpful to review some of the characteristics and themes that are prevalent in our postmodern context.

Four Characteristics of Postmodernism in Relation to "the New Poverty"[5]

As we seek to identify the claims of postmodernity upon the Christian missional priorities, it is worth reflecting upon four key distinctive shifts that currently shape our understanding of the culture within which Western culture now exists. First is the decline of the West as the primary

---

2. Inbody, "Postmodernism," 524.

3. Eco, *Name of the Rose*, 65.

4. Adams, "Toward a Theological Understanding."

5. These are elaborated upon in Bauman, *Intimations of Postmodernism*, 35–52, 96–101. See also Cooper, "Reformed Apologetics," 109–10.

reference for what constitutes "normative" in economic indicators. With the birth of multinational globalism after the fall of the Berlin wall, the rise of China as a serious player in the free market, WTO protests, Naomi Klein's *No Logo*, and the formalization of the European Union with its inclusion of Eastern Bloc countries within its Western capitalist economic system, the world has become much larger and much smaller at the same time. While the force of the U.S. in the world market remains a dominant (at times domineering) reality, the number of viable decision markets has increased not merely in name but in practice. In short, cultural and national boundaries are eroding to the point of becoming merely public relations theory.

Secondly, there is a legitimization/authority crisis whereby the challenge faced in the midst of the postmodern turn has been finding an authoritative voice from which to reconcile contrary and/or differing views. In regard to the economic questions facing the new poverty, rather than being a threat to stable economic indicators, this proves both a challenge and opportunity to allow other voices to enter into the dialogue and the democratic conclave of voices to arise where authority is not merely invested through having the largest GNP. When Jesus asked the question "Who do you say that I am?" he was raising the question of authority.

Thirdly, taking into account the rise of the intellectual marketplace, we have moved from Karl Marx's critique of capitalism, which argued that one needs only look to the means of production to understand where true economic power lies. As the world has moved out of the industrial age of the Victorian period and into the twenty-first century, the value of "intellectual property" has transformed the marketplace and tipped the economics of the world to where, as was seen with the rise of the dot.com era in the late 1990s. The value of ideas over products has fully dawned. This is potentially an incredible opportunity for the majority world, where the go-to-market speed has increased and the ability to bring ideas to investors continues to be a viable trade option.

Fourthly, the process of deconstruction and return to "connectedness" means a revisioned sense of what it means to have a self in the twenty-first century. This is discussed by Shin Kuk-Won, professor of philosophy at Chongshin University in Seoul, Korea, in his article "Postmodernism and a Christian Response,"[6] where he asserts that the centrist view of the

6. See Kuk-Won, "Postmodernism," 17–18.

world where there is one dominate locus of thought has evaporated under the rejection of Enlightenment presuppositions of classical metaphysical thought. That the individual self precedes the communal (I am before we are), and that reason is the prior and dominate form of testing truth claims over experience, is now being challenged. While the term "deconstruction" may send a chill up the spine of some people, as seen in the conversation partners throughout this book it is certainly providing a renewed opportunity to philosophically and theologically reject the assumption of human autonomy in favor of "connectedness," which models two dominant metaphors in the New Testament—the kingdom of God and the body of Christ—and a return toward a serious concern for the practical ethical aspects of human life.

Given this shift away from Western economic and philosophical dominance and toward a more diffused global economic platform, Scripture does provide some important guidelines that provide vectors for establishing a measuring line for what God values in relation to our economic view of the world:

God owns all things. As we hear in Psalm 24: 11 and Job 41:11, the notion of personal and corporate ownership is an illusion. We have a lease relationship with this life. The fact that people in the U.S. speak of "owning" a home, when the truth of the matter is that a vast majority of so-called homeowners are tenants in a residence owned by a mortgage company or bank, shows how far we have come as a culture into the illusion that debt can be equated with ownership. This mentality has seeped into the marrow of our understanding of God's ownership of creation and all that dwells in it. Regardless of the stance on free will and human ethical agency, it is central to the Christian story that God is not only the sustainer of creation, but the owner as well. We are "stewards" of the garden, not owners. As John Taylor points out in his book *Enough Is Enough,*

> Only in his unbroken awareness of God is man's [*sic*] technological mastery safe. Only in his acceptance of creaturehood can his dominion [over creation] be prevented from becoming raw domination. For being answerable to God, man remains answerable for his fellow creatures and for the soil of his earth.[7]

God provides all things. As Scripture reminds us, there is no need for anxiety (Matt 6; Luke 12: 22–31), no need for love of money (Heb 13:5), no need to serve two masters (Matt 6:24), no need to seek sec-

7. Taylor, *Enough Is Enough*, 53.

ondary treasures (Matt 13:45). In short, what is needed is provided for—all the rest is fuel for fear at best. Part of the concerns surrounding economic flux in the global market and the rash responses—from Y2K paranoia to increased interest in Middle East oil reserves—has to do with a need to manage and control those things we need due to our deep lack of faith. In short, we pay lip service to God's providence the more we hoard goods and services unto ourselves at the expense of others. The notion that we are to "focus on our family" as a primary concern only exacerbates the divide between our nuclear family and the "widow and orphan" whose caring is not additive, but central to our understanding of what the kingdom of God looks like.

We release all things. Henri Nouwen spoke prophetically by saying that the only true prayer is the prayer offered with open hands. Jesus' ministry was one of freedom for hospitality through our availability to others. In this way, the extreme is the normative—we are to sell all, give all, and ultimately receive all as pure gift, as we hear in Luke 12:33–34 and Mark 10:21, 29–30. To "hold on" and grasp things is harmful—both to one's relationship with God (e.g., the "eye of the needle," Luke 18:18–24) and to one's own identity and relations with others, as we hear in 1 Timothy 6:8–10. It is important to remember that the judgment upon Sodom and Gomorrah was a judgment primarily based upon a lack of hospitality— they had become so consumed with feeding their own lusts and desires that they had no time nor vision to acknowledge the needs of others. In this understanding, we do not stand apart *from* Sodom, but *in* the Sodom town square.

We are called to desacralise all things. Jacques Ellul in *The Technological Society*[8] argued that money in and of itself carries the power to allure and as such we can imbue it with idol-like passion. In this way money according to Ellul has power in and of itself, and we need to act counter to this temptation and set people and relationships in primary consideration as having priority over things. In this way we need to work toward a redefinition of the Good Life: defined not by quantity of things but by quality of relations. As we are challenged under the divine command ethics of the Ten Commandments, we are not to mission any other God than God, *period*. To hold things and the monetary value we have placed upon those things above drawing people close in relationship with ourselves

---

8. Ellul, *Technological Society*.

and their Creator is to choose graven images. This goes for the notion of usury or putting interest upon money borrowed from others. As we hear in 2 Corinthians 8, we are challenged not to coerce more money from people but liberate people from addiction and release people from debts. The work of the One.org campaign is not merely fad, it is a mandate. As we learn from liberative and emancipatory theologies, God's concern for the poor is primary throughout Scripture. "The new poverty" is the poverty of ignorance to the cry from the margins. Theologian Ron Sider reminds us, "Are the people of God truly God's people if they oppress the poor? Is the church really the church if it does not work to free the oppressed? [Regarding Matt 25:41] The meaning [of Matt 25] is clear and unambiguous. Jesus intends that disciples imitate his own special concern for the poor and needy. Those who disobey will experience eternal damnation. . . . Regardless of what we do or say at 11am on Sunday morning, affluent people who neglect the poor are not the people of God. . . . God is not neutral. His freedom from bias does not mean that he maintains neutrality in the struggle for justice. He is indeed on the side of the poor."[9] What are some of the challenges that remain before us in striving toward an authentic and humble biblical economics? We are reminded of the Lausanne Covenant: "All of us are shocked by the poverty of millions and disturbed by the injustices which cause it. Those of us who live in affluent circumstances accept our duty to develop a simple lifestyle in order to contribute more generously to both relief and evangelism."[10] In many respects, little has changed in the thirty years since the Covenant was drafted, but the challenge before us as people of integrity is still there.

The Challenge of the Church Is to Develop into a "Missional Community of Loving Defiance"

Ron Sider puts it this way in *Rich Christians in An Age of Hunger*: "The church should consist of communities of loving defiance. Instead it consists largely of comfortable clubs of conformity. A far-reaching reformation of the church is a prerequisite if it is to commit itself to Jesus' mission of liberating the oppressed."[11] There is a need for intentionality among the faithful to form a new vision of the church as "communities of loving

9. Sider, *Rich Christians*, 70–71.
10. "Lausanne Covenant," article 9.
11. Sider, *Rich Christians*, 200.

defiance" in a world moving with the inertia of consumerism and an ego-born appetite that shows no natural hope of slowing. The time for a spiritual reassessment of economics and the new poverty, where the deficits of the soul are acknowledged on the balance sheet alongside the deficits of the checkbook, in now needed. Bonhoeffer made this all too apparent as a factor for authentic discipleship:

> Earthly possessions dazzle our eyes and delude us into thinking that they can provide security and freedom from anxiety. Yet all the time they are the very source of anxiety. If our hearts are set on them, our reward is an anxiety whose burden is intolerable. . . . When we seek security in possessions we are trying to drive out care with care, and the net result is the precise opposite of our anticipations.[12]

What are some helpful points to actively reflect on? Ron Sider in *Rich Christians in an Age of Hunger* uses these criteria for decisions regarding a kingdom-centric economics:

1. Does this purchase move toward a globally sustainable personal lifestyle?

2. How am I distinguishing between necessities and luxuries in my economic priorities?

3. Work toward eliminating "status expenditures"—can a used car to the work or a new one?

4. Work toward distinguishing between expenditures for creativity and recreation and excessive self-indulgence.

5. Try to encourage expenditures on occasional special celebrations rather than when the whim hits you—i.e., plan ahead for spending.

6. Strive toward severing the connection between what you earn and what you consume. This is by far the most difficult task for many. The reality that downsizing is incredibly difficult shouldn't surprise anyone—but the call to do so is certainly central to our faith.

In closing, the challenge before the kenotic self as someone missionally open and desiring to live a missionally radical life is to live out an economic program that draws from both a Philippians and Colossians perspective. In the letter to the Philippians there is that marvelous and

12. Bonhoeffer, *Cost of Discipleship*, 154–57.

breathtaking description of Christ, the son of God, who gave up all aspirations to power in order to be servant of all, emptying (*kenosis*) himself on the cross, as we saw in chapter 1 of this book. Ministry in the city and the workplace is about being servant to everyone—the equalizing power of respect. That is the micro focus of economic responsiveness to the new poverty, where we begin from a kenotic stance by "emptying" and thereby freeing ourselves from the debt that binds, and walking into the world free to give and free to receive.

The letter to the Colossians speaks of Christ who is the head of all things and in whom all things hold together. He is the head of the new creation, the church. He is the one who has reconciled all things to himself through the cross. He is the hope of glory within us. Ministry in the city, across the rural countryside, around the family dining table, in the narthex of the church, and walking into the workplace is about seeing Jesus as Lord of the city and the systems as well as the individuals—the empowering vision that means there are no exclusion zones for Christian presence and influence, working to see the "powers that be" honor the God by whom and for whom they are created. That is the macro focus of ministry. We acknowledge with confidence that the world is God's and all that dwells in it—there are no owners, we are all "leasing agents" in creation. As such, we claim the right for marginalized voices in the global market to be not only heard but listened to, and their words acted upon.

Ultimately, we need to have our collective eyes and ears on both the Philippians paradigm and the Colossians mandate as the kenotic self. This is living in true stereophonics and responsive economics. It is in the tension of the micro and macro needs of the coming kingdom of God that we are indeed called and certainly cared for by the gifting hand of God.

9

The Kenotic Self amidst the Secular City

O NE OF THE GREAT challenges before a revised missiological paradigm is the question of secularization—can we speak of the mission
of God as truly secular people? This question presupposes a couple of
thoughts: first, that the gospel of Jesus Christ is a deeply "secular" message
not confused nor constrained in the ongoing categorical battles within
the church regarding "in the world but not of it"; secondly, that to be a
Christian reborn in Christ's image and to truly state "it is not I who live
but Christ who lives in me" is to make a deeply "secular" claim. In this way
I am taking the gospel accounts at their word *as* the Word of God—that
the Word became Flesh and dwelt among us. This is the heart of secularization—that the world becomes palpably real and thereby cosmopolitan
instead of mythical and overtly idealized. To continue to struggle against
the secular is to fight the incarnation of God and limit God's in-breaking
and redeeming power in the world.

Dietrich Bonhoeffer has called the rise of the secular as "man's coming of age" and the dismissal and disenchantment of God's rightful place.
But secularization is neither the end of Christianity nor the swan song of
authentic mission. As we have seen in the preceding chapters, the movement of the kenotic self as missionally open and given for the world aligns
with many Continental thinkers as well as contemporary theologians. As
we shall discuss in this chapter, this turn toward embracing diversity as
part of God's character and therefore living ethically within communities of loving defiance is a call to ethics that has awakened in twenty-first
century culture not an outright dismissal of God as modernist writers on
mission have feared, but a renewed humility toward God's missiological
working both in the world now and in the world yet to come. In short, we
now must speak about God in secular fashion if we are to speak of and
with God at all.

The Kenotic Self amidst the Secular City

Harvey Cox and The Secular City

The dominant shape that secularization has taken in the twenty-first century is that of urbanization. As many urbanists[1] have stated before, as Christians we have left the garden and are headed for the city, the New Jerusalem. The urban is the shape of the new society and does not only refer to the city. To put it another way, the *secular* in the form of the *urban* means a structure of common life in which, as Harvey Cox prophetically announced over forty years ago, the "diversity and the disintegration of tradition are paramount."[2] As Cox points out in *The Secular City*, the urban city denotes a double edged challenge—identity that gives way to impersonality but also tolerance, instead of long-term acquaintances and traditional moral sanctions. The continued challenge for the proclamation of the gospel in a secular form such as the urban city is this tension whereby identity is grounded in a community context, which is accelerated and occasional, prior to their own-self understanding, which is deep (going back to our discussion of Augustine in chapter 2) and constant. This is ironic in such individualistic times and yet the rise in people seeking help with feelings of isolation and loneliness in areas where club memberships are at an all-time high is just one of many indicators to consider. Cox goes on to note that in addition to this form of secularization as urbanization is the rise in the late twentieth century of the "technopolis." In Cox's paradigm, the technopolis superseded town, which itself superseded tribe. When we speak of individuals in today's secular cities, we are speaking of the "technopolitan"—a networked subject who is not bound to myths of the tribe anymore, and neither to the struggle between personal bonds of blood and law in the *polis*.

According to Cox, there are at least three origins of secularization to be found in the Bible that call mankind to maturity: *creation* as the disenchantment of nature, *the Exodus* as the desacralisation of politics, and *the Sinai Covenant* as the deconsecrating of values. As he goes on to state in *The Secular City*, "Secularization is the liberation of man from religious and metaphysical tutelage, the turning of his attention away from other worlds and towards this one."[3] In this regard, the radical turn toward deep attentiveness to one's lived life that secularization offers is

---

1. See Bakke, *Urban Christian*.

2. Cox, *Secular City*, 18.

3. Ibid., 31.

not the end of Christian belief but rather the logical consequence of biblical faith. As people who sit under the authority of Scripture, it is right that we should map our course in the world based upon the plotline and radical trajectory of Creation, the Exodus, and the Sinai Covenant, which continually pushes us into secular lives before and with a Holy God who stands amidst, not apart from, the secular.

The Shape of Mission for the "Glocal Secular"—Anonymity and Mobility

Figuring a responsive and attentive missiologically secular repose as the kenotic self calls for an embrace of some key factors that have often been seen as anathema to the authentic proclamation of the gospel. This is the heart of the "glocal" (global yet local) secular city. First, we must challenge the notion that *anonymity* is essentially a bad thing. Part of the journey of the kenotic self is to release our expectations as to how people will make community. For many hurt and battered by disappointment or pain, anonymity is a means of observation before commitment—a chance to know before they are known. I have worked with too many churches that continue to ask visitors who attend a morning service to stand up, be recognized or even to wear a badge identifying themselves as a visitor so that members (read: those who are "in") can greet them. This can be as violating to new visitors as a strip search in a parking lot—a breach of personal space not for their benefit, but for our sense of knowing who people are in our space and our desire for control. What anonymity calls us to remember is that it is not the job of visitors to announce themselves and be labeled accordingly. No, it is the role of the community of loving defiance to wait, be hospitable, and create a space of care and compassion where people can announce themselves. Church representatives therefore cannot come to these people seeking to know whether they are "one of us" now and if not, then they must leave. Rather, they must respect anonymity in the first instance and therefore need a theology of anonymity whereby we allow space for the other to be. Martin Buber's I-Thou[4] encounter, which we can use for our close friends, must be replenished by an I-You encounter, which loves the other but keeps the distance for a time and allows them to move near to us when they are ready, not when we demand it.

---

4. Buber, *I and Thou.*

Second, *mobility* is something that is to be embraced and reflected upon rather than blindly found antithetical to the gospel. In a more extended article I have written about the "sacredly mobile adolescent,"[5] the generation that is growing up in our midst who find mobility as something normative—fluidity in information sharing, quick transit between cultures, and seamless switching back and forth through media options whether it is streaming video, mash-up music selections, or photo merging. Mobility is also not new nor is it to be seen purely as a impediment toward deep and meaningful identity formation. The poor and the marginalized have seen mobility not only as the lack of ability to locate a home, but as a means of discovery and willingness to work with the land (in rural settings) as well as collaborate with other groups and build alliances. The powerful try to stop mobility and label it as a problem. The theological implication of mobility is to be found in the Old Testament: the Hebrews were nomads; the prophets did not preach in their own country; when the people of Israel were abroad in Babylon, they did not lose their belief but strengthened it; God moved in the Ark of the Covenant and was not very happy about David wanting to build a temple. In the New Testament, this mobility continues onward, likened to a rushing wind in Acts 2 that answers Jesus' injunction to "go" at the end of Matthew's Gospel. Yet since the rise of organized and encultured Christendom after Constantine in the fourth century there has been a subtle settling down that has left much of the established mainline church in a static repose to the world, represented more by still empty buildings that show what has been rather than the quickened hearts of converts pointing to what should and will be. In this time, the slow death of Christendom is now the opportunity to become mobile again. As seen in the constant movement of the Trinity and the ever deepening call to heed the voice within ourselves after Augustine, the kenotic self holds a humble repose toward the anonymity and mobility of others and seeks to find ways of "going out" as Jesus mandated in Matthew 28 as a normative posture in the world.

The Style of the Secular—Pragmatic and Profane

Two of the qualities inherent to today's secular polis are a value for the *pragmatic* and a humble acknowledgement that life is *profane* even amidst the sacred. Today's secular self does not ask for mystery, myths, and meta-

---

5. See Keuss and Willett, "Sacredly Mobile Adolescent."

physics alone. The framing principle is voiced in a basic query: "Will it work?" Despite the rise in spiritual inquisitiveness as seen in our discussion of neo-paganism in earlier chapters, twenty-first-century culture is also an era post-ontological yet deeply functional. In the Old Testament, God is not described primarily in an ontological way ("I am that I am") but by what he did for, with, and through Israel. Saint Paul writes to the Colossians that God in Christ holds the world together and that this is not our job alone. Christ is the truth; we should likewise do the truth. This is to reframe the notion that the goal of the Christian life is not merely to have faith in Christ; rather, we are to have the faith of Christ as well—living out in pragmatic ways before the world the faith into which we have been called and call others to. This is in keeping with our earlier reflections on the work of Emmanuel Lévinas where the primary question of philosophy should not be ontology but ethics. How we live in the world is ultimately what we belief, and everything resides on this assertion.

In addition to the pragmatic, the secular polis is boldly *profane*—that is to say, it is lived outside the temple and in this world. Much of what has galvanized the form of Christianity the church has inherited can be traced to the destruction of the temple in Jerusalem under Titus in 70 AD. This destruction moved the energy of those Jewish converts to the Christian faith into community with the pagan converts with seismic force—there was no turning back. Yet there are those who still seek the sacred and secular line to be drawn at the church door, presupposing that God is somehow more present in one location as opposed to the streets, the alleyways, the barrios, the office complexes on the other side of the stain glass vista. The "profane," as we may label it, is part of a creation that God deemed "good" in Genesis, although it is now largely fallen under abandonment to sin. This is a world that is worth redeeming as are the people who populate it. In short, this is a call to open our eyes wider, forgo the lines of demarcation between what we deem as the realms of sacred and profane, and seek instead the proximity of God's work as a call for social change. This is to move with free mobility and pragmatic concern as the kenotic self to embrace the deeply incarnate God found in the seemingly profane world whose face is Jesus Christ and dwelling with us as the Holy Spirit in the secular realm.

The Kenotic Self and a Missional Theology of Social Change

"The starting point for any theology of the church today must be a theology of social change."[6] Cox wrote *The Secular City* after spending a year living in Berlin in the 1960s only a few months after the Berlin Wall was erected. He would drive back and forth through Checkpoint Charlie every morning and watch how a city divided by the wall developed into East and West. In Cox's mind the question was fairly basic: was God more present on one side of the Wall than the other? Yet what are the more profound walls that humanity continues to erect and separate people, divide communities, and ultimately cut people off from one another? In an article in The Christian Century forty years after the publication of *The Secular City*, Cox again asserted that even with the fall of the Berlin Wall, the central thesis of the book remains as fresh as ever:

> The thesis of *The Secular City* was that God is first the Lord of history and only then the Head of the Church. This means that God can be just as present in the secular as in the religious realms of life, and we unduly cramp the divine presence by confining it to some specially delineated spiritual or ecclesial sector. This idea has two implications. First, it suggests that people of faith need not flee from the allegedly godless contemporary world. God came *into* this world, and that is where we belong as well. But second, it also means that not all that is "spiritual" is good for the spirit. These ideas were not particularly new. Indeed, the presence of the holy within the profane is suggested by the doctrine of the incarnation—not a recent innovation. As for suspicion toward religion, both Jesus and the Hebrew prophets lashed out at much of the religion they saw around them. But some simple truths need restating time and again. And today is surely no exception.[7]

Just as much as Cox spoke years ago to the consequences of walls dividing communities and thereby attempting to segregate the realms of God's purview into locales of sacred and secular, these are words to be reflected upon today. We are called to this life, to this world. This is the context and shape of our mission and outreach, and therefore our mission is a deeply secular and urbanely informed one. Trying to fulfill that task, we should not forget the kingdom of God that is in process of realizing itself in this place, with these people who surround us and walk with on

6. Cox, *Secular City*, 117.

7. Cox, "Secular City 25 Years Later," 1026.

the highways and byways of the secular polis. The kingdom of God is always coming and we are to contribute to the announcing of this coming kingdom (Mark 1:15).

It was Karl Marx in the nineteenth century who concluded that the only way for change in an ever increasing technopolis is catastrophe and revolution. Yet Marx's revolution was only for the here and now and was constrained by the limits of the human imagination, and therefore has repeatedly failed in the generation since his grand manifesto. As we discussed with Derrida and his notion of "rupture" that breaks through and releases us toward new possibilities, rather than a limited and broken revolution born from humanity, the true holy rupture announced through Scripture and located in the ministry of Jesus is the kingdom of God itself, which sets everything anew. It is this rupture through and with the kingdom lived fully by the people of God in the midst of the secular world that is the home of the church, gathered around the feet of the risen Christ and not merely singing about him.

The Church as God's Avant-Garde

To embrace the reality of the secular shape of mission in the technopolis is to also be weary of the temptation to see only the shape of the secular as opposed the content that God's desires to redeem—that is, humanity and the created order. Primarily, the church is not an institution *per se* nor a catalogue of doctrines, but people who are to embody the kingdom of God, which is creation-shaped and grounded and empowered by God. In this regard, the institutional church must enable people to participate in God's action in the world and follow Christ. The characteristics of this is participation in and for the world. The contour of the participation in and for the world God therefore desires to redeem is accented by authentic and radical embodied expressions of *kerygma* (proclamation), *diakonia* (service), and *kiononia* (community).

Kerygma

"To believe the kerygma is to believe that man not only could but should have dominion over the earth."[8] Under the new régime called the kingdom of God, humanity comes to maturity (Gal 4). History is now placed somewhere between Easter and the end of all things; it is a constant struggle

---

8. Ibid., 141.

between the old régime of dehumanizing powers and the new régime of humanity binding itself to God through Christ's mercy and the Spirit's empowerment. To be missionally open to the world is to radically open our lives in acts of praise and vocation to and with our God. To believe the kerygma is to proclaim in word and deed the truth of God's reconciling power for the world now and yet to come.

Diakonia

As Cox makes clear, "the church has the responsibility to be the servant and the healer of the city."[9] The place and purpose of the kenotic self are entwined in the call to bind the wounds of the secular, to announce the year of the Lord's favor (Isa 61), and walk humbly with our God toward such vital horizons. The churches must come back to the secular—not as development aid somehow safely removed, but as co-sojourners.

Koinonia

To be the church is to be authentically hospitable, that is, fellowship (koinonia) becomes the sign and seal of Christ's "hope made visible."[10] This was articulated well by Johannes C. Hoekendijk (1912–75) from Holland. While with the World Council of Churches, Hoekendijk was closely involved in theological discussions in the ecumenical movement and contributed much to its thinking. Hoekendijk was a vehement critic of the church-centric view of mission. In his thinking, the world and the kingdom of God (kergyma) are correlated. The kingdom of God is destined for the world. The world is the field in which the seeds of the kingdom are sown—the scene of the proclamation of the kingdom. The kerygma of the early Christians did not know of a redemptive act of God that was not directed to the whole world. In the New Testament, the world as a unity is confronted with the church as "the avant-garde of God," or what Rudolph Bultmann called the "eschatological community." For Hoekendijk, it is God–world–church and not God–church–world. He wrote:

> As soon as we speak of God, we are also bringing into speech the world as God's theatre stage for his action, and it is foremost the Church who knows it and who will respect it. As soon as the Church acknowledges God, she also admits her own implicitly ec-

9. Ibid., 145.
10. Ibid., 156.

centric position, hoping that at some point in time it may come true that she can serve as an instrument to honor the world's worth and destiny. The eccentric Church cannot insist on protecting its own structures. She does not possess a private sociology; rather she uses—purely functionally—all available worldly structures in so far as they are useable.[11]

"Church" is nowadays the place where the church's functions (*kerygma, diakonia, koinonia*) occur in the sense of an abolition of religious and cultic boundaries. As Cox notes in *The Secular City*, "Jesus Christ comes to his people not only through ecclesiastical traditions, but through social change."[12]

The Church as Cultural Exorcist

Another task before the kenotic self in a missionally open repose in and amidst the secular is that of cultural exorcist. As Cox states, "Mission is, in a sense, the neurosis of cultures; secularization corresponds to maturation."[13] Jesus liberated humanity from the demonic reality that enslaved it, as well as from the imagination of a dominating legal system. This is what church should do today. But new social systems require new church structures. Secular people do not define themselves by where they live but by what they are or where they work. The residential parish is now only one possibility of church in secular age. Universities, hospitals, public schools, town halls and other locales offer gathering points for reasoning, bridge building, and commitment to social change that were once considered to be areas not in the purview of the church. Yet in a culture that is at times seeking some anonymity prior to belonging and sees mobility as an opportunity rather than a problem, these examples represent areas of encounter and commitment in ways the parish is not. These communities do not need to be a permanent institution and therefore offer places ready to respond with fluidity. They have an *ad hoc* character that mirrors much of the secular shape around anonymity and mobility as well as pragmatisim, and they can engage life in the midst of the profane rather than ignore it. In this mode of partnership with such institutions, the church acknowledges that it does not, nor was it ever called to, have all the tools for repairing the social problems of our world. Christians can

11. Quoted in Thomas, *Classic Texts*, 191–92.
12. Cox, *Secular City*, 159.
13. Ibid., 164.

and should struggle side by side with non-Christians to achieve a world where humanity can find healing and wholeness, as well as being a witness to the Christ who calls all people to this wholeness through the work of the cross—as Cox states, by partnering with rather than taking away the work of the secular.

The Vox Humana *as the Voice of the* Imago Dei: *To Speak in a Secular Fashion of God*

In 1944, Dietrich Bonhoeffer wrote rather prophetically in one of his letters from prison:

> We are proceeding toward a time of no religion at all. . . . How do we speak of God without religion . . . ? How do we speak in a secular fashion of God? . . . The movement beginning about the thirteenth century . . . towards the autonomy of man . . . has in our time reached a certain completion. Man has learned to cope with all questions of importance without recourse to God as a working hypothesis. . . . [Traditionally "missional"] efforts are made to prove to a world thus come of age that it cannot live without the tutelage of "God." Even though there has been surrender on all secular problems, there still remain the so-called ultimate questions— death, guilt—on which only "God" can furnish an answer, and which are the reason why God and the Church and the pastor are needed. . . . But what if one day they no longer exist as such, if they too can be answered without "God"?[14]

As Bonhoeffer muses, "How do we speak in a secular fashion of God?" The mandate for the kenotic self is to enter the secular as Christ did so fully through his incarnated life and ministry. As Christians we cannot refuse speaking of God (for this is the nature of the Good News) and therefore speak, as Bonhoeffer states, "in a secular fashion." When we speak of God, we do not speak *about* God. Speaking *of* God means to name God. To name God is to use language, personal language, and the language of our social background. Thus speaking of God is a deeply *sociological* opportunity—finding the shape of God in the secular as well as articulating the fullness of God that is apostolic and catholic. We cannot talk about God in a general sense alone but must strive to do so in a deeply contextual one. This is the task before the kenotic self: to remain in a missionally open engagement in and for the world that allows its heart to break with that which breaks the heart of God amidst this secular age.

14. Bonhoeffer, "Ultimate Questions," 251.

10

The Kenotic Self after the Eucharist

THIS CONCLUDING CHAPTER OFFERS both a synthesis of the proceed-
ing discussion as well as a commissioning of the kenotic self to be
"on-the-way in the field of paths," to use Martin Heidegger's phrase to
denote a posture of humility and openness to and for the world we are
called to. As Heidegger saw that only by walking amidst the woods would
a woodpath be made evident, so it is for the kenotic self as one formed
by the culture, drawn outward for the world from within, forged and
grounded in identity in deep responsibility for the other as Jesus directed
in his Great Commandment, and released into the world as one freely
and fully "given"; we must see the form of our mission arise only after
being on-the-way of being in the secular and sent into it. In this way, the
"paths" formed in being missionally open will lead toward what I have
called a "poetic cartography of grace," where one can orient oneself and
be invited to search for the nexus of the subject and the sacred—to touch
the wounds and truly believe—becoming missionally reflective by being
in the world actively and authentically. Using the analogy of map making,
where the traditional understanding of cartography is that of mapping
space on a two-dimensional field of north–south–east-west, I am arguing for the kenotic self as one who is known in a "poetic cartography
of grace" where the "mapping" is not merely of spaces within the world
for evangelism, but the very fullness of space and time itself—in short, a
mapping of meaning that is always renewed and creatively re-imagined,
as exhibited in the missional project of Lesslie Newbigin and Dietrich
Bonhoeffer. Seeing a missionally open posture in the world as a poetic
cartography of grace encourages outreach and evangelism that is fully
embodied and embodies both in the message and the messenger—you
are in Christ as Christ is in you. This "missionally open mapping" has
no boundary or edge that would announce the end of the world, or a

limit to the universe that creates a sense of beginning and end, but is fully enclosed and three-dimensional, moving itself in the fullest breath, depth, and height of time and space as one who comes unannounced and bears Gospel—Good News.

In a 1766 pastoral letter, John Wesley offers the following advice, which stands as a provocative mission statement for the kenotic self in the contemporary world:

> The spark of faith which you have received is of more value than all the world. O cherish it with all your might! Continually stir up the gift that is in you, not only by continuing to hear [God's] word at all opportunities, but by reading, by meditation, and above all by private prayer. Though sometimes it should be a grievous cross, yet bear your cross and it will bear you. . . . Surely His grace is sufficient for you.[1]

The challenge of the kenotic self today continues to be the challenge and opportunity to provoke Christians to be the sign and seal of the "spark of faith" that is "continually stirred up" in and for each new generation as a testimony to God's sufficient grace. Like many generations beforehand, this is a generation in Western culture in need of evocative encounters that "continually stir up" a deep and abiding faith that seeks understanding and practice in the world. In my teaching as well as pastoral ministry, much of my work and passion is focused upon removing impediments that can hinder individuals from fully seeking God with all their heart, mind, soul, and strength. My vision as a teacher and researcher is to encourage faith as the authentic experience of being sought out by God in a community of fellow sojourners that is actively evocative.

This vision of the kenotic self articulated in the preceding chapters acknowledges the responsibility of the church to be missionally open to the world through furnishing a *sense of place* that is immanently hospitable to the diverse ethnic and cultural expressions found in the contemporary world at large. Parker J. Palmer, in his book *To Know as We Are Known: Education as a Spiritual Journey*, framed a wonderful picture of this sense of place drawn from his reading of the desert father Abba Felix. To paraphrase Palmer, evocative ministry is the act of *creating a space in which truth is practiced through community.*[2]

1. Wesley, "Letter to Mrs. Woodhouse," 201.
2. See Palmer, *To Know* and *Courage to Teach.*

Carving out such a space is vital for ministry and mission grounded in the Christian faith. The deep aspects of this space are well-defined as a space of learning and reflection that includes:

- deep reading of *Scripture* (the touchstone and definitive authority on matters of faith and practice);

- a renewed introduction to the fullness of the *Christian tradition* (to acknowledge our roots in the ancient church and see the lives of early church leaders where biography reflects theology);

- *reason* that is sharpened and challenged throughout the world in which the church exists (where critical thought encourages the ordering of evidence of revelation and guards against poor reading of Scripture and life); and

- learning that is grafted to lived *experience* in the world (toward the development of a personal experience of faith that becomes a communal confession and witness through praxis).

These fence posts define a dynamic frontier by which Christian faith and mission can assert its character and vision with integrity to the community theologically, historically, and pastorally.

As a teacher and pastor, I view the task of radical proclamation of the gospel as never fulfilled when confined merely to the pulpit, lecture hall, or classroom. To paraphrase Emil Brunner's oft-quoted statement, "we exist by active participation in the world as a fire exists by burning." Dietrich Bonheoffer restated this well when reflecting that the evidence of deep theological reflection is living in the world and "taking life in one's stride, with all its duties and problems, its successes and failures, its experiences and helplessness." He goes on to say, "it is in such a life that we throw ourselves utterly into the arms of God and *participate* in his sufferings in the world and watch with Christ in Gethsemane."[3] In this way, the Great Commission of Jesus in Matthew 28 is also the Great Death of the Church as we know it in a contemporary setting. We have to let go of ourselves, let go of our expectations and plans for mission in order to be compelled by the true mission of God's radical love for the world. Reciprocally, the Christian community is informed, challenged, humbled, ministered to, and redeemed through its active participation in the world as it throws

---

3. Bonhoeffer, *Prisoner of God*, 169; emphasis added.

itself "utterly into the arms of God and *participates* in his sufferings." By losing ourselves and listening to the other , we may finally find that which we have always sought for—the embrace of God in the embrace by and with the world that God loves with complete abandon.

Additionally, I see some of William Willimon's insights from his book *Worship as Pastoral Care*[4] as a welcome vision and reminder of what the goal is of radically missional ministry that affirms and encourages individuals to be sojourners of faith in the world in which they live and breathe.

First, provoke an awareness of the holy in all manners of life.

A dynamic missional community has the unique opportunity through a variety of worship and discipling encounters to bring clear focus to life through the integration of faith and lived life. Here the church is to challenge members within a missional community to view life as an act of worship that is *a continual, timeless act of character* and not merely an ephemeral moment found in a designated chapel time or trapped only within a Sunday liturgy.

John Drury challenges us to rethink the way we view worship, in that it

> needs to be something more than religion as so far achieved and organized. It will even have to be something opposed to the confidence mixed with possessive restlessness of such religion, if it is to save religious people from tight circles their religions get themselves into. If it posits a center. . . . It will have to be a center in which breaking and giving away is at least permanently at work as joining and holding. There is an image of it in the central rite of Holy Communion: the focal "body" of Christ broken and given.[5]

Second, invite members of the faith community to a dialogue with eternal hope through the question, "What is God's intention toward you?"

While it is assumed by some that the self-selection of the church fellowship denotes a fairly uniform understanding and commitment to Christian faith, this is not always the case. Many individuals and families coming to a church on Sunday are unsure as to God's intentions and have not experienced a witness to the trustworthiness and goodness of God's character. Where an awareness of the holy encourages the community

---

4. Willimon, *Worship as Pastoral Care.*

5. Drury, *Pot and Knife,* 4–5.

to see God as *present* in the world, a dialogue with eternal hope aims at showing God's presence as not merely immutable, but *actively righteous* and desirous of righteous response. I continue to be challenged by this opportunity to create a context where church members and students, both from deeply churched backgrounds and those from post-Christian backgrounds, can hear anew Wesley's words that surely "His grace is sufficient for you."

Third, to be a kenotic self is to continually nurture the vocational quest.

Where a dialogue with providence provokes the question, "What is God's intention *toward* you?," the nurturing of the *vocational* quest asks the community the question, "What is God's intention *for* and *with* you?" Frederick Buechner's oft-quoted view of vocation continues to be a challenge:

> It comes from the Latin *vocare*, to call, and means the work a man [*sic*] is called to by God. There are all different kinds of voices calling you to all different kinds of work, and the problem is to find out which is the voice of God rather than of Society, say, or the Superego, or Self-Interest. By and large a good rule for finding out is this. The kind of work God usually calls you to is the kind of work *(a)* that you need most to do and *(b)* that the world most needs to have done.... Neither the hair shirt nor the soft berth will do. *The place God calls you to is the place where your deep gladness and the world's deep hunger meet.*[6]

Nurturing an awareness of "the place where your deep gladness and the world's deepest hunger meet" is a core focus of ministry that awakens the deep sense of calling, and is a central charge for my vision for the seminary community as a body that calls out individuals to dwell in the world with a compassionate resolve for the sake of the gospel.

Last, communicate the theological ideas of acceptance and forgiveness embodied in God's grace that gives the freedom to relate to God honestly and with the assurance that God will not turn from us amidst doubts, fears, or questions.

This is particularly relevant when viewing mission as essentially a teaching ministry—helping others learn about the very nature of God's love for them. As a faculty member working directly with university stu-

---

6. Buechner, *Wishful Thinking*, 95; emphasis added.

dents interested in finding their sense of calling in the world, I have found it vital to encourage those moving into ministry in the church to create conversations and listen deeply to those they are called into relationship with. Henri Nouwen in his book *Creative Ministry* wrote that more often than not, ministry can become a "violent process" rather than a redemptive one. He states it in the following way:

> "Getting things under control" is what keeps most teachers and students busy, and a successful teacher is often the individual who creates the conviction that man [*sic*] has the necessary tools to tame the dangerous lion he is going to face as soon as he leaves the training field. . . . *As long as teaching takes place in this context it is doomed to be a violent process and evoke a vicious cycle of action and reaction in which man faces his world as new territory that has to be conquered but is filled with enemies unwilling to be overruled by a stranger.* The teacher who enters this arena is forced to enter into a process which by its nature is competitive, unilateral, and alienating. *In short: violent.*[7]

In contrast to this notion, the call of the kenotic self is a call to the task of encouraging those learning about the Christian faith to see the life of the gospel as an inherently *redemptive* process where the communication of the gospel is *evocative* rather than competitive, *bilateral* rather than unilateral, and *actualizing* rather than alienating.

In his novel *The Once and Future King*, T. H. White provides a description of the purpose and hope of learning as Merlyn speaks of his role as a teacher and mentor to a young King Arthur who is but a leader in the making:

> "The best thing . . . ," replied Merlyn . . . "is to learn something. That is the only thing that never fails. You may grow old and trembling in your anatomies, you may lie awake at night listening to the disorder of your veins, . . . you may see the world around you devastated by evil lunatics, to know your honor trampled in the sewers of baser minds. There is only one thing for it then—to learn. Learn why the world wags and what wags it. This is the only thing which the mind can never exhaust, never alienate, never be tortured by, never fear or distrust, and never dream of regretting."[8]

---

7. Nouwen, *Creative Ministry*, 5–6; emphasis added.

8. White, *Once and Future King*, 183.

In short, the compelling vision for mission in today's contemporary world is one that offers an arena where community members can "learn why the world wags and what wags it."

In summary, my vision for the kenotic self is the humble framing of identity as enfolded in the Great Commandment of Jesus whereby one is truly responsible for the other and fully given to the world. In this regard, Christian community shaped around the kenotic call of Christ is this compelling space for authentic dialogue in response to alternative forms of community offered today in society. This is the heart of authentic community—people committed to the gospel where the community participates in dynamic hospitality through a heartfelt exchange of lives where deep questions can be addressed in an environment of acceptance and forgiveness. Such a provoking space where obedience to truth can be practiced through community rekindles that "spark of faith" which we have received and "is of more value than all the world."

The kenotic self is one that will always "overflow the institution" of theology as identity in truth escapes categories. To be captured and compelled by the gravity of God's grace is to be propelled into a deeply abiding way of life that finds its very form exhibiting the qualities of a re-imagined incarnation of the Christ in the world. As St. Paul writes in the second letter to the Corinthians, it is deep within the Christian story to figure this face where

> we all, who with unveiled faces contemplate the Lord's glory, are being transformed into his image with ever-increasing glory. . . . For God, who said, "Let light shine out of darkness," made his light shine in our hearts to give us the light of the knowledge of God's glory displayed in the face of Christ. (3:18; 4:6)

This is a shaping and employment of mission after the kenotic self that takes its form through a retrieval of Jesus' words at the institution of the Eucharist:

> When the hour came, Jesus and his apostles reclined at the table. And he said to them, "I have eagerly desired to eat this Passover with you before I suffer. For I tell you, I will not eat it again until it finds fulfillment in the kingdom of God."
>
> After taking the cup, he gave thanks and said, "Take this and divide it among you. For I tell you I will not drink again of the fruit of the vine until the kingdom of God comes."

And he took bread, gave thanks and broke it, and gave it to them, saying, "This is my body given for you; do this in remembrance of me." (Luke 22:14–19)

The directive of Jesus for this remembrance is a creative act as seen in verse 19 where the "do this" of remembrance recalls *poiesis*, which is the root of "poetics." Such is the act of remembrance that a missional theology of openness proposes and is the heartbeat of the kenotic self. In the same way, such a dynamic missional theology invites us to come, as St. Paul wrote, "with unveiled faces [to] contemplate the Lord's glory [and be] transformed into his image with ever-increasing glory" (2 Cor 3:18). Such is the invitation to "do this"—*poiesis*—in remembrance of him.

Bibliography

Adams, Daniel J. "Possibilities for Theology in the Postmodern Era." *Asia Journal of Theology* 10 (April 1996) 89–104.

———. "Toward a Theological Understanding of Postmodernism." *Cross Currents* 47.4 (1997–98) n.p. Online: http://www.crosscurrents.org/adams.htm.

Altizer, Thomas J. J. *The Contemporary Jesus*. New York: SUNY Press, 1997.

Aristotle. *Nicomachean Ethics*. Translated by W. D. Ross. New York: World Library Classics, 2009.

Augustine. *Confessions*. Translated by Garry Willis. New York: Penguin, 2006.

———. "De vera Religione [On True Religion]." In *Augustine: Early Writings*, translated by John H. S. Burleigh, 218–83. London: SCM, 1953.

Baker, Jonny, and Doug Gay. *Alternative Worship: Resources from and for the Emerging Church*. Grand Rapids: Baker, 2004.

Bakke, Ray. *The Urban Christian*. Downers Grove, IL: InterVarsity, 1999.

Bal, Mieke. *Reading "Rembrandt": Beyond the Word-Image Opposition*. Cambridge New Art History and Criticism. Cambridge: Cambridge University Press, 1991.

Baudrillard, Jean. *Jean Baudrillard: Selected Writings*. Edited by Mark Poster. London: Polity, 1988.

———. "Simulacra and Simulation." In *Jean Baudrillard: Selected Writings*, edited by Mark Poster, 166–84. London: Polity, 1988.

Bauman, Zygmunt. *Intimations of Postmodernity*. London: Routledge, 1991.

Berry, Philippa, and Andrew Wernak, editors. *Shadow of Spirit: Postmodernism and Religion*. London: Routledge, 1992.

Bettelheim, Bruno. *The Uses of Enchantment: The Meaning and Importance of Fairy Tales*. New York: Vintage, 1989.

Bonhoeffer, Dietrich. *The Cost of Discipleship*. Translated by Reginald Fuller. New York: Touchstone, 1995.

———. *Life Together*. Translated by Reginald Fuller. New York: HarperCollins, 1978.

———. *Prisoner of God: Letters and Papers from Prison*. Translated by Reginald Fuller. New York: Macmillan, 1971.

———. "The Ultimate Questions." June 8, 1944. In *Prisoner of God: Letters and Papers from Prison*, translated by Reginald Fuller, 145–49. New York: Macmillian, 1971.

Bourdieu, Pierre. *Distinction: A Social Critique of the Judgment of Taste*. Translated by Richard Nice. Cambridge: Harvard University Press, 1984.

Bosch, David. *Transforming Mission: Paradigm Shifts in Theology of Mission*. Maryknoll, NY: Orbis, 1991.

Boyd, Gregory A. *God of the Possible: A Biblical Introduction to the Open View of God*. Grand Rapids: Baker, 2000.

Bibliography

Browning, Don S. *A Fundamental Practical Theology: Descriptive and Strategic Proposals.* Minneapolis: Fortress, 1991.

Buber, Martin. *I and Thou.* Translated by Walter Kaufmann. Edinburgh: T. & T. Clark, 1970.

Buechner, Frederick. *Wishful Thinking: A Theological ABC.* New York: Harper & Row, 1973.

Burke, John Patrick. "The Ethical Significance of the Face." *ACPA Proceedings* 56 (1982) 194–206.

Cassier, Ernst. *Rousseau Kant Goethe.* Princeton: Princeton University Press, 1945.

Cohen, Richard. "Emmanuel Lévinas: Happiness Is a Sensational Time." *Philosophy Today* 25 (1981) 196–203.

Cooper, John W. "Reformed Apologetics and the Challenge of Post-Modern Relativism," *Calvin Theological Journal* 28 (1993) 109–10.

Coppola, Francis Ford. Quoted in *Glasgow Film Theatre Bulletin*, March 1999.

Cox, Harvey. *The Secular City.* New York: Macmillan, 1965

———. "The Secular City 25 Years Later." *The Christian Century*, November 7, 1990, 1025–29.

Cronin, Kevin. *Kenosis: Emptying Self and the Path of Christian Service.* London: Continuum, 2005.

Derrida, Jacques. "'This Strange Institution Called Literature': An Interview with Jacques Derrida." In *Acts of Literature*, edited by Derek Attridge, 33–75. New York: Routledge, 1992.

———. *Writing and Difference.* Translated by Alan Bass. London: Routledge, 1978.

Descartes, Rene. *Meditations.* Vol. 2 of *The Philosophical Works of Descartes.* Translated by Elizabeth S. Haldane and G. R. T. Ross. New York: Cambridge University Press, 1981.

Dodridge, Anna. "I am not involved in the Emergent Church." Online: http://www.emergingchurch.info/stories/annadodridge/index.htm.

Donato, Eugenio, and Richard Macksey, editors. *The Structuralist Controversy: The Languages of Criticism and the Sciences of Man.* Baltimore: Johns Hopkins University Press, 1972.

Drury, John. *The Pot and the Knife.* London: SCM, 1979.

Eco, Umberto. *The Name of the Rose.* Translated by William Weaver. San Diego: Harcourt Brace Jovanovich, 1989.

Ellul, Jacques. *The Technological Society.* Translated by John Wilkinson. New York: Vintage, 1964.

Elmer-DeWitt, Philip. "Cyberpunk!" *Time*, February 8, 1993. Online: http://www.time.com/time/magazine/0,9263,7601930208,00.html.

Emergent Village. Online: http://www.emergentvillage.us/about/.

Endo, Shusaku. *A Life of Jesus.* Translated by Richard Schuchert. New York: Paulist, 1978.

———. *Silence.* Translated by William Johnson. New York: Taplinger, 1980.

Evans, C. Stephen, editor. *Exploring Kenotic Christology: The Self-Emptying of God.* Oxford: Oxford University Press, 2006.

Fairbairn, A. M. *The Place of Christ in Modern Theology.* London: Hodder & Stoughton, 1895.

Fee, Gordon D. "The New Testament and Kenosis Christology." In *Exploring Kenotic Christology: The Self-Emptying of God*, edited by C. Stephen Evans, 25–44. New York: Oxford University Press, 2006.

Bibliography

Feenstra, Ronald. "Reconsidering Kenotic Christology." In *Trinity, Incarnation, and Atonement: Philosophical and Theological Essays,* edited by Ronald J. Feenstra and Cornelius Platinga Jr., 128–52. Notre Dame: University of Notre Dame Press, 1989.

Feinberg, John S. *No One Like Him: The Doctrine of God.* Wheaton, IL: Crossway, 2001.

———. "Unqualified Divine Temporality." In *God and Time: Four Views,* edited by Gregory E. Ganssle, 187–213. Downers Grove, IL: InterVarsity, 2001.

Flores, Aaron. "An Exploration of the Emerging Church in the United States: The Missiological Intent and Potential Implications for the Future." MA thesis, Vanguard University, 2005.

Forsyth, P. T. *The Person and Place of Jesus Christ.* 1961. Reprinted, Eugene, OR: Wipf and Stock, 1996.

Foster, Hal. *The Return of the Real.* Cambridge, MA: MIT Press, 1996.

Frame, John M. *No Other God: A Response to Open Theism.* Phillipsburg, NJ: P & R, 2001.

Fretheim, Terence E. *The Suffering of God: An Old Testament Perspective.* Overtures to Biblical Theology. Philadelphia: Fortress, 1984.

Garvie, Alfred E. *Studies in the Inner Life of Jesus.* New York: Doran, 1907.

Geisler, Norman L., and H. Wayne House. *The Battle for God: Responding to the Challenge of Neo-theism.* Grand Rapids: Kregel, 2001.

Glasser, Arthur. *Announcing the Kingdom: The Story of God's Mission in the Bible.* Grand Rapids: Baker Academic, 2003.

Goethe, Johann Wolfgang von. *Goethe—the Collected Works* Edited by Douglas Miller. Scientific Studies 12. Princeton: Princeton University Press, 1995.

———. "On Morphology—the Purpose Set Forth." In *Goethe—the Collected Works,* edited by Douglas Miller, 63–67. Scientific Studies 12. Princeton: Princeton University Press, 1995.

———. *Wilhelm Meister's Apprenticeship and Travels.* Translated by Thomas Carlyle. 2 vols. London: Chapman & Hall, 1858.

Gore, Charles. *The Incarnation of the Son of God: Being the Bampton Lectures for the Year 1891.* London: Scribner, 1891.

Gorman, Michael. *Inhabiting the Cruciform God: Kenosis, Justification, and Theosis in Paul's Narrative Soteriology.* Grand Rapids: Eerdmans, 2009.

Guder, Darrell L. "From Mission and Theology to Missional Theology." Inaugural lecture as Henry Winters Luce Professor of Missional and Ecumenical Theology, Princeton Theological Seminary, December 4, 2002.

———, editor. *Missional Church: A Vision for the Sending of the Church in North America.* The Gospel and Our Culture Series. Grand Rapids: Eerdmans, 1998.

———. "Missional Church: From Sending to Being Sent." In *Missional Church: A Vision for the Sending of the Church in North America,* edited by Darrell L. Guder, 1–17. The Gospel and Our Culture Series. Grand Rapids: Eerdmans, 1998.

Guignon, Charles, editor. *The Cambridge Companion to Heidegger.* London: Cambridge University Press, 1998.

Hall, Christopher A., and John Sanders, *Divine Debates: A Dialogue on the Classical and Openness Views of God.* Grand Rapids: Baker, 2002.

Harvey, David. *The Condition of Postmodernity: An Enquiry into the Origins of Cultural Change.* Oxford: Blackwell, 1989.

Heim, S. Mark. *The Depth of the Riches: A Trinitarian Theology of Religious Ends.* Grand Rapids: Eerdmans, 2001.

Bibliography

Hiebert, Paul G. "Evangelism, Church, and Kingdom." In *The Good News of the Kingdom: Mission Theology for the Third Millennium*, edited by Charles Van Engen et al., 153–61. Maryknoll, NY: Orbis, 1993.

Hornby, Nick. *31 Songs*. London: Penguin, 2003.

Hunsberger, George, and Craig Van Gelder, editors. *The Church between Gospel and Culture: The Emerging Mission in North America*. The Gospel and Our Culture Series. Grand Rapids: Eerdmans, 1996.

Husserl, Edmund. *Cartesian Meditations: An Introduction to Pure Phenomenology*. Translated by Dorion Cairns. Boston: Nijhoff, 1960.

Hyppolite, Jean. *Logic & Existence*. New York: SUNY Press, 1997.

Inbody, Tyron. "Postmodernism: Intellectual Velcro Dragged Across Culture." *Theology Today* 57 (1995) 524–38.

John Chrysostom. *Homily on Philippians*. Quoted in *Ancient Christian Commentary on Scripture*, vol. 8, edited by Mark J. Edwards, 217–89. Downers Grove, IL: InterVarsity, 1999.

Jones, E. Stanley. *A Song of Ascents: A Spiritual Autobiography*. Nashville: Abingdon, 1968.

Joyce, James. *A Portrait of the Artist as a Young Man*. 1914. Reprint, New York: Vintage, 1993.

Keuss, Jeffrey F. *A Poetics of Jesus: The Search for Christ through Writing in the Nineteenth Century*. Ashgate New Critical Thinking in Theology & Biblical Studies. London: Ashgate, 2002.

———. "Seeing and Being with Youth: *Bildungsroman* and Coming of Age from Goethe to *Star Wars* and *The Matrix*." *Journal of Youth and Theology* 5.2 (2006) 29–48.

———, and Rob Willett. "The Sacredly Mobile Adolescent—A Hermeneutic Phenomenological Study toward Revising of the Third Culture Kid Typology for Effective Ministry Practice in a Multivalent Culture." *Journal of Youth Ministry* 8.1 (2009) 7–24.

Kuk-Won, Shin. "Postmodernism and a Christian Response." *Pro Rege* 22.4 (1994) 15–25. Online: http://www.dordt.edu/publications/pro_rege/crcpi/95097.pdf.

"The Lausanne Covenant (July 1974)." Appendix 3 in *Evangelizing Neopagan North America*, by Alfred C. Krass, 189–97. Institute of Mennonite Studies Missionary Studies 9. Scottdale, PA: Herald, 1982.

Levi-Strauss, Claude. *The Savage Mind*. Chicago: University of Chicago Press, 1966.

Lévinas, Emmanuel. *Ethics and Infinity: Conversations with Phillipe Nemo*. Translated by Richard Cohen. Pittsburgh: Duquesne University Press, 1985.

———. *Otherwise than Being, or, Beyond Essence*. Translated by Alphonso Lingis. Boston: Nijhoff, 1981.

———. *Totality and Infinity: An Essay on Exteriority*. Translated by Alphonso Lingis. Pittsburgh: Duquesne University Press, 1969.

Lingis, Alphonso. Translator's introduction in *Otherwise than Being, or, Beyond Essence*, by Emmanuel Lévinas, xvii–xlv. Boston: Nijhoff, 1981.

Macksey, Richard, and Eugenio Donato, editors. *The Structuralist Controversy: The Languages of Criticism and the Sciences of Man*. Baltimore: Johns Hopkins University Press, 1972.

Maddox, Randy L. *Responsible Grace: John Wesley's Practical Theology*. Nashville: Abingdon, 1994.

Mallonee, Bill. "Double Cure." *V.O.L.*, by Vigilantes of Love. Warner/WEA compact disc B000002N9F. © 1996 by Warner/WEA.

Bibliography

Marion, Jean-Luc. *Being Given: Towards a Phenomenology of Givenness.* Translated by Jeffrey L. Kosky. Stanford: Stanford University Press, 2002.

—. *God without Being.* Translated by Thomas A. Carlson. Chicago: University of Chicago Press, 1991.

—. *In Excess: Studies of Saturated Phenomena.* New York: Fordham University Press, 2002.

The Matrix. DVD. Written and directed by Andy and Lana Wachowski. 1999; Burbank, CA: Warner Home Video, 2007.

Matsuoka, Fumitaka. "The Christology of Shusaku Endo." *Theology Today* 39 (1982) 294–99.

McCarthy, Cormac. *The Crossing.* London: Picador, 1994.

McLaren, Brian. *More Ready Than You Realize.* Grand Rapids: Zondervan, 2002.

Milbank, John, Catherine Pickstock, and Graham Ward, editors. *Radical Orthodoxy: A New Theology.* London: Blackwell, 1998.

Moltmann, Jürgen. *Theology of Hope: On the Ground and the Implications of a Christian Eschatology.* Translated by James W. Leitch. 1967. Reprint, Minneapolis: Fortress, 1993.

Moore, Stephen D. *Mark and Luke in Postructuralist Perspectives: Jesus Begins to Write.* New Haven: Yale University Press, 1992.

Morrissey, Lee. "Derrida, Algeria, and 'Structure, Sign, and Play.'" *Postmodern Culture* 9.2 (1999) n.p.

Morse, Christopher. *Not Every Spirit: A Dogmatics of Christian Disbelief.* Valley Forge, PA: Trinity, 1994.

Muller, Richard A. *God, Creation, and Providence in the Thought of Jacob Arminius: Sources and Directions of Scholastic Protestantism in the Era of Early Orthodoxy.* Grand Rapids: Baker, 1991.

Nouwen, Henri. *Creative Ministry.* Garden City, NY: Image, 1978.

Nussbaum, Martha. *The Fragility of Goodness: Luck and Ethics in Greek Tragedy and Philosophy.* 2nd ed. Cambridge: Cambridge University Press, 2001.

Palmer, Parker J. *The Courage to Teach: Exploring the Inner Landscape of a Teacher's Life.* San Francisco: Jossey-Bass, 1998.

—. *To Know as We Are Known.* San Francisco: HarperCollins, 1993.

Pattison, Stephen. "Some Straw for the Bricks." In *The Blackwell Reader in Pastoral and Practical Theology*, edited by James Woodward and Stephen Pattison, 133–45. London: Blackwell, 2000.

Pinker, Steven. *How the Mind Works.* New York: Norton, 1997.

Pinnock, Clark H. "Evangelical Theology in Progress." In *Introduction to Christian Theology*, edited by Roger A. Badman, 75–85. Louisville: Westminster John Knox, 1998.

—. *Most Moved Mover: A Theology of God's Openness.* Grand Rapids: Baker, 2001.

—, et al. *The Openness of God: A Biblical Challenge to the Traditional Understanding of God.* Downers Grove, IL: InterVarsity, 1994.

Plato. *Phaedrus.* In *The Collected Dialogues of Plato*, edited by Edith Hamilton, 475–525. Princeton: Princeton University Press, 1961.

Raschke, Carl. *The Next Reformation: Why Evangelicals Must Embrace Postmodernity.* Grand Rapids: Baker, 2004.

Redfield, Marc. *Phantom Formations: Aesthetic Ideology and the Bildungsroman.* Ithaca, NY: Cornell University Press, 1996.

Bibliography

Röder-Bolton, Gerlinde. *George Eliot and Goethe: An Elective Affinity*. Studies in Comparative Literature 13. Amsterdam: Rodopi, 1998.

Rovira, Jim. "Baudrillard and Hollywood: Subverting the Mechanism of Control and *The Matrix*." Online: http://www.ubishops.ca/BaudrillardStudies/vol2_2/rovira.htm.

Rushdie, Salman. "Is Nothing Sacred? An Interview with Salman Rushdie." *Granta* 31 (Spring 1990) 98–111.

Sanders, Cheryl. *Ministry at the Margins: The Prophetic Mission of Women, Youth & the Poor*. Downers Grove, IL: InterVarsity, 1997.

Sanders, John. *The God Who Risks: A Theology of Providence*. Downers Grove, IL: InterVarsity, 1998.

Schäfer, Martin. "The Sacred: A Figureless Figure: On Heidegger." Paper presented at the Conference on Theology and Criticism, Johns Hopkins University, March 4–7, 1998.

Schleiermacher, Friedrich D. E. *On Religion: Speeches to Its Cultured Despisers*. Cambridge: Cambridge University Press, 1988.

Seel, John. "Meet Your Neighborhood Neo-pagan." *Re:generation Quarterly* 3.4 (1997) 16–22.

Sider, Ron. *Rich Christians in an Age of Hunger*. London: Hodder & Stoughton, 1990.

Solzhenitsyn, Aleksandr. "The Relentless Cult of Novelty and How It Wrecked the Century." *New York Times Book Review*, February 7, 1993, 3, 17.

Song, Choen-Seng. *Third Eye Theology: Theology in Formation in Asian Settings*. Maryknoll, NY: Orbis, 1979.

Star Wars: Episode I—The Phantom Menace. DVD. Written and directed by George Lucas. 1999; Los Angles: 20th Century Fox, 2005.

Sterling, Bruce. *Mirrorshades: The Cyberpunk Anthology*. New York: Arbor House, 1986.

Tallon, Andrew. "Intentionality, Intersubjectivity, and the Between: Buber and Lévinas on Affectivity and the Dialogical Principle." *Thought* 53 (1978) 292–309.

Taylor, Charles. *Sources of the Self*. Cambridge: Harvard University Press, 1989.

Taylor, John. *Enough Is Enough: A Biblical Call for Moderation in a Consumer-Oriented Society*. Minneapolis: Fortress, 1977.

Taylor, Mark C. *Erring*. Chicago: University of Chicago Press, 1984.

Templeton, Douglas A. *The New Testament as True Fiction: Literature, Literary Criticism, Aesthetics*. Playing the Texts 3. Sheffield: Sheffield Academic, 1999.

Thomas, Norman E., editor. *Classic Texts in Mission and World Christianity*. London: Orbis, 1993.

Tiessen, Terrance. *Providence & Prayer: How Does God Work in the World?* Downers Grove, IL: InterVarsity, 2000.

Tillich, Paul. *The Protestant Era*. Translated by James Luther Adams. Chicago: University of Chicago Press, 1948.

———. *Über die Idee einer Theologie der Kultur*. Berlin: Reuther & Reichard, 1919.

Tracy, David. *The Analogical Imagination: Christian Theology and the Culture of Pluralism*. London: SCM, 1981.

Turkle, Sherry. *Life on the Screen: Identity in the Age of the Internet*. New York: Simon & Schuster, 1997.

Verkuyl, Johannes. *Contemporary Missiology: An Introduction*. Grand Rapids: Eerdmans, 1978.

Ward, Graham. *Christ and Culture*. Oxford: Blackwell, 2005.

Bibliography

Ware, Bruce A. *God's Lesser Glory: The Diminished God of Open Theism*. Wheaton, IL: Crossway, 2000.

Warren, Rick. *The Purpose Driven Life: What on Earth Am I Here For?* Grand Rapids: Zondervan, 2002.

Webb, William J. *Slaves, Women & Homosexuals: Exploring the Hermeneutics of Cultural Analysis*. Downers Grove, IL: InterVarsity, 2001.

Webber, Robert. *Ancient-Future Faith: Rethinking Evangelicalism for a Postmodern World*. Grand Rapids: Baker, 1999.

Wesley, John. "Letter to Mrs. Woodhouse." Dated May 17, 1766. In *The Letters of the Rev. John Wesley*, edited by John Telford, 5:11–12. London: Epworth, 1931.

White, T. H. *The Once and Future King*. New York: Ace, 1987.

Williams, Mark B. *Endo Shusaku: A Literature of Reconciliation*. London: Routledge, 1999.

Willimon, William H. *Worship as Pastoral Care*. Nashville: Abingdon, 1979.

Wolff, Robert Paul. *Kant's Theory of Mental Activity: A Commentary on the Transcendental Analytic of the Critique of Pure Reason*. Cambridge: Harvard University Press, 1963.

Yancey, Philip. "Japan's Faithful Judas: Shusaku Endo's Struggle to Give His Faith a Japanese Soul." *Books and Culture*, January–February 1996, 3, 6–7.

You've Got Mail. DVD. Directed by Nora Ephron. 1998; Burbank, CA: Warner Home Video, 1999.

Zizioulas, John D. *Being as Communion: Studies in Personhood and the Church*. Crestwood, NY: St. Vladimir's Seminary Press, 1985.

Index of Names and Subjects

Index of Names and Subjects

Index of Names and Subjects

Index of Names and Subjects

Index of Scripture

Printed in Great Britain
by Amazon